Optimizing and Troubleshooting Hyper-V Networking

Mitch Tulloch with
the Windows Server Team

PUBLISHED BY
Microsoft Press
A Division of Microsoft Corporation
One Microsoft Way
Redmond, Washington 98052-6399

Copyright 2013 © Mitch Tulloch with the Windows Server Team

All rights reserved. No part of the contents of this book may be reproduced or transmitted in any form or by any means without the written permission of the publisher.

Library of Congress Control Number (PCN): 2013938862
ISBN: 978-0-7356-7900-9

Printed and bound in the United States of America.

First Printing

Microsoft Press books are available through booksellers and distributors worldwide. If you need support related to this book, email Microsoft Press Book Support at mspinput@microsoft.com. Please tell us what you think of this book at *http://www.microsoft.com/learning/booksurvey*.

Microsoft and the trademarks listed at http://www.microsoft.com/about/legal/en/us/IntellectualProperty/Trademarks/EN-US.aspx are trademarks of the Microsoft group of companies. All other marks are property of their respective owners.

The example companies, organizations, products, domain names, email addresses, logos, people, places, and events depicted herein are fictitious. No association with any real company, organization, product, domain name, email address, logo, person, place, or event is intended or should be inferred.

This book expresses the author's views and opinions. The information contained in this book is provided without any express, statutory, or implied warranties. Neither the authors, Microsoft Corporation, nor its resellers, or distributors will be held liable for any damages caused or alleged to be caused either directly or indirectly by this book.

Acquisitions Editor: Anne Hamilton
Developmental Editor: Karen Szall
Project Editor:
Editorial Production: Jean Trenary
Technical Reviewer:
Copyeditor: Megan Smith-Creed
Indexer:
Cover:

Contents

Introduction 6

Hyper-V networking tips 11

    Best practices 11

    VLAN concepts and troubleshooting 12

    MAC addresses and virtual guests 13

    Network card drivers 14

    Example: Intel Teaming NIC driver and VMQ 15

Monitoring network performance 16

    Physical network adapters 21

    Virtual network adapters 21

    Virtual switch 22

Virtual switch 28

    System event log 29

    Performance counters 30

    Diagnostic event log and packet capture 30

    Packet capture within vmswitch 31

Port mirroring 34

MAC addresses 38

    Duplicate MAC addresses 39

    MAC address behavior during live migration 40

    Duplicate MAC addresses on a standalone host 41

    Duplicated MAC addresses due to address range overlapping 42

Single Root I/O Virtualization 43

    How SR-IOV works 44

    Enabling SR-IOV 46

    Enabling the guest operating system 49

    Implementing network redundancy 50

    Troubleshooting SR-IOV 51

N_Port ID Virtualization 57

Failover cluster networking 66

    Resiliency 66

    Network Quality of Service 67

    SMB Multichannel 69

    NetFT 69

SMB Multichannel and CSV 70

    The new way: Windows Server 2012 cluster network roles and metrics 71

    How SMB Multichannel changes the behavior to select the CSV cluster network 74

Multitenant networking: Single cluster 76

    Option 1: Consolidated network (single NIC team) 77

        Requirement 1: Redundancy 78

        Requirement 2: Communication isolation 78

        Requirement 3: Performance 79

    Option 2: Multiple physical networks (many teams) 80

        Requirement 1: Redundancy 80

        Requirement 2: Communication isolation 81

        Requirement 3: Performance 81

Multitenant networking: IaaS environment 82

    Scenarios 83

    Physical separation 83

    Layer 2 and Layer 3 isolation 85

    NIC Teaming 88

Virtual Machine Queue 91

Hyper-V Replica 93

Network Virtualization 105

    Step 1: Check that each virtual machine has the same VirtualSubnetId 107

    Step 2: Check that the lookup records are correct on each host for the
virtual machines 108

Step 3: Check that a WNV subnet gateway address exists on each host for the virtual machines 109

Step 4: Check that a WNV route exists on each host for each subnet in the virtual machine network 110

Step 5: Check that each virtual machine's host has the same provider address that was specified in the lookup records 110

Step 6: Check that the provider routes are correct on each host 111

Step 7: Check that each host has Network Virtualization bound to a network adapter 112

Putting it all together 113

Use Windows PowerShell to display configuration 116

    Get-NetVirtualizationLookupRecord 116

    Get-NetVirtualizationCustomerRoute 117

Tracing VmSwitch and WNV 119

    Following packets routed through WNV 119

    Troubleshooting dropped packets 120

Enable debug logging in System Center 2012 VMM SP1 121

VMM DHCP Server tracing 122

Automating network settings for hosts 125

Client Hyper-V 130

The problem 130

The solution 130

Introduction

Troubleshooting is a difficult art to learn because it requires deep knowledge of the subject of study, familiarity with a wide variety of tools, and thinking that can be both sequentially logical and inspirationally outside the box. Perhaps the best way of learning such arts is by watching experts demonstrate their skills as they are exhibited in different situations.

Optimizing how something performs can also be quite difficult to master. If you've ever used an old-fashioned radio where you had to find your station using a dial, you'll realize that a certain degree of fiddling is required to tune things just right. Now imagine a device that has dozens of dials, each tuning a different variable, with all the variables related to one another so that tuning one affects the settings of the others. Tuning an information technology system can often be just like that...or worse!

Optimizing and Troubleshooting Hyper-V Networking is all about watching the experts as they configure, maintain, and troubleshoot different aspects of physical and virtual networking for Hyper-V hosts and the virtual machines running on these hosts. And when I use the word "expert" here, I really mean it, because the contributors to this book all work at Microsoft and have first-hand knowledge and experience with the topics they cover. The different sections in this book range from how to automate the network configuration of Hyper-V hosts using Windows PowerShell to get it right the first time so you won't have to troubleshoot, to step-by-step examples of how different networking problems were identified, investigated, and resolved.

Of course there's no way to exhaustively or even systematically cover the subject of optimizing and troubleshooting Hyper-V networking in a short book like this. But I hope that by reading this book (or by referring to certain topics when the need arises) your own troubleshooting skills will become more finely honed so you will be able to apply them more effectively even in scenarios that are not described in this text.

This book assumes that you are a moderately experienced administrator of the Windows Server virtualization platform. You should also have at least a basic understanding of Windows PowerShell and familiarity with tools and utilities for managing Windows servers, Hyper-V hosts, virtual machines, and the various components of an enterprise networking infrastructure.

The main focus of this book is on the Windows Server 2012 version of Hyper-V and associated networking capabilities. Some content in this book may also be applicable for earlier versions of Hyper-V and Windows Server, and we've tried to indicate this wherever applicable.

Good luck in mastering this arcane art!

—*Mitch Tulloch, Series Editor*

About the contributors

Cristian Edwards Sabathe is the EMEA Regional Workload Lead for Server Virtualization based in Barcelona, Spain. Cristian has over five years of support and virtualization experience and has a deep technical hands-on experience with Hyper-V and SCVMM since Windows 2008. He is a Subject Matter Expert in the WW Microsoft Virtualization team and content creator of Workshops for Premier and MCS customers. Together with the SCOM PFE Diego Martinez Rellan, he is also the author of the *Hyper-V Management Pack Extensions* available from http://hypervmpe.codeplex.com. Cristian's contributions to the community can be found on his personal blog at http://blogs.technet.com/cedward and in the World Wide PFE virtualization blog at http://blogs.technet.com/virtualpfe.

Jason Dinwiddie is a Senior Consultant with Microsoft Consulting Services. Jason is an eight-year veteran at Microsoft as a Senior Consultant for State and Local Government. With 16 years of overall IT experience, Jason is focused on virtualization, management, and private cloud, specializing in Hyper-V.

Jean-Pierre R M de Tiege is a Senior Technologist for Charteris (http://www.charteris.com) currently working at Microsoft on the Government Gateway team as a build manager. Jean-Pierre has worked in a variety of fields over the last 14 years, from e-learning to e-commerce, and has worked with Microsoft technology since the first .NET version came out, initially in the Netherlands but now full time in the United Kingdom.

Jeff Stokes is a Senior Premier Field Engineer (PFE) at Microsoft. Jeff has been in the IT industry for 19 years, initially cutting his teeth at DEC and climbing the system administrator ladder from there. He regularly posts to his popular TechNet blog "Dude Where's My PFE?" which can be found at http://blogs.technet.com/b/jeff_stokes/.

Keith Hill is a Senior Support Escalation Engineer with the Windows Server Core High Availability Team. Keith started his Microsoft journey in 1999 on the afterhours support team. He moved to the cluster team about seven years later, and two year ago became the Support Topic Owner for Hyper-V within Commercial Technical Support (CTS). Keith would like to thank **John Howard**, Program Manager for Hyper-V, for his assistance in writing the SR-IOV section of this book. Keith would also like to thank **Tina Chapman**, a Lab Engineer with the US-CSS CC lab group, for her assistance in writing the NPIV section of this book.

Madhan Sivakumar is a Software Development Engineer II (SDE II) in Windows Core Networking at Microsoft. Madhan graduated from the University of Florida in 2008 and joined Microsoft as a developer in the Windows Core Networking team. In Windows 7, he worked on implementing network Quality of Service in the Windows networking stack. In Windows 8, he was part of the Hyper-V networking team and was responsible for improving network diagnostics in the Hyper-V environment. He also implemented features like VM QoS and IPSec task offload support for virtual machines in Windows Server 2012. His LinkedIn profile can be found at http://www.linkedin.com/in/madhansivakumar.

Mark Ghazai is a Data Center Specialist with Microsoft U.S. State and Local Government (SLG) team. His goal is to address challenging issues within SLG customer datacenters and their journey toward private and public cloud adoption. Assisting customers to get a deeper understanding of managed and consolidated datacenters powered by Windows Server 2012, Windows Server 2012 Hyper-V, Remote Desktop, VDI, and System Center 2012 suite, along with Microsoft Identity Management Solutions (FIM, UAG, TMG) is his main area of focus. Before this role, he was a Senior Premier Field Engineer (PFE) and Senior Support Escalation Engineer for several years. His TechNet blog can be found at http://blogs.technet.com/mghazai.

Nick Eales is a Senior Premier Field Engineer at Microsoft, based in Sydney, Australia. Nick has 17 years of industry experience, with the last eight of those years at Microsoft. Within Microsoft, Nick has worked on multiple teams focusing on Core Platforms support, Failover Clustering and Hyper-V, and currently is the architect for the Hyper-V Risk Assessment Program and one of the leads for the Failover Clustering Risk Assessment Program.

Shabbir Ahmed is a Partner Enterprise Architect (Infrastructure) with the Partner Enterprise Architect Team (PEAT). Shabbir helps Microsoft partners build hosting solutions. He is best in working with partners/customers to link and apply complex technologies to their business strategies and continues to be a creative thinker with high energy and enthusiasm. Apart from Microsoft Certifications he was Microsoft MVP from 2011 to 2013 and holds multiple certifications including CCIE, CEH, and ISO 27001 LA. His LinkedIn profile can be found at http://in.linkedin.com/pub/shabbir-ahmed/58/575/209.

Subhasish Bhattacharya is a Program Manager for Clustering and High Availability at Microsoft. He has worked at Microsoft at for seven years in multiple teams including High Availability and Clustering and Core Networking (DNS). His LinkedIn profile can be found at http://www.linkedin.com/pub/subhasish-bhattacharya/1/a75/b0.

Thomas Roettinger is a Program Manager in the Partner and Customer Ecosystem Team at Microsoft and works with technologies like Hyper-V and System Center Virtual Machine Manager. His team runs the Windows Server TAP Program and collects very early technology best practices. Before he joined the Product Group he was the EMEA Virtualization Lead in Microsoft Premier Field Engineering. During this time he was responsible for various services such as the Hyper-V Risk Assessment Program and the Implementing Hyper-V Workshop. He has rich experience in cloud implementations across various business segments such as hosters and enterprises. Thomas maintains a personal blog at http://blogs.technet.com/b/cloudytom and also contributes to his team blog at http://blogs.technet.com/b/wincat.

Tim Quinn is a Support Escalation Engineer on the Windows Platform Distributed Systems Networking team. He delivers reactive support for Microsoft Networking technologies such as DNS, DHCP, Remote Access, and core network connectivity, including troubleshooting of Hyper-V Network Virtualization.

Trevor Cooper-Chadwick is a Principle Consultant with Microsoft Consulting Services UK. A Subject Matter Expert in the WW Microsoft Virtualization team, he is passionate about helping customers architect and deploy highly effective infrastructure solutions leveraging both private and public cloud technologies and services. An IT veteran with many years of experience spanning Internet, Grid, and High Performance Computing, he has spent the last five years defining and building leading-edge solutions using Hyper-V, System Center Virtual Machine Manager and Azure.

About the companion content

The companion content for this book consists of a zip file containing the Windows PowerShell scripts found in certain sections of this title. This companion content can be downloaded from the following page:

http://aka.ms/TroubleshootHyper-VNetworking/files

Acknowledgments

Thanks to Anne Hamilton and Karen Szall at Microsoft Press, to Megan Smith-Creed our copy editor, and to Jean Trenary for production services.

Errata & book support

We've made every effort to ensure the accuracy of this content and its companion content. Any errors that have been reported since this content was published are listed on our Microsoft Press site at oreilly.com:

http://aka.ms/TroubleshootHyper-VNetworking/errata

If you find an error that is not already listed, you can report it to us through the same page.

If you need additional support, email Microsoft Press Book Support at mailto:mspinput@microsoft.com.

Please note that product support for Microsoft software is not offered through the addresses above.

We want to hear from you

At Microsoft Press, your satisfaction is our top priority, and your feedback our most valuable asset. Please tell us what you think of this book at:

http://aka.ms/tellpress

The survey is short, and we read every one of your comments and ideas. Thanks in advance for your input!

Stay in touch

Let's keep the conversation going! We're on Twitter: http://twitter.com/MicrosoftPress.

Hyper-V networking tips

Windows Server 2012 includes a number of new and enhanced features that can help reduce networking complexity while lowering costs, simplifying management tasks, and delivering services reliably and efficiently. While we'll be digging into how to optimize and troubleshoot some of these different features later in this book, we're going to start with some best practices for Hyper-V networking and a few troubleshooting tips that Hyper-V administrators might find handy. Jeff Stokes, a Senior Premier Field Engineer working at Microsoft, leads the way in the following section.

Windows Server 2012 Hyper-V networking

Hyper-V in Windows Server 2012 brings out some amazing new functionality in networking. For Windows administrators who aren't used to troubleshooting network switches, this can be intimidating. Troubleshooting networks in Hyper-V is fairly similar to troubleshooting any other network issue as long as the administrator remembers to treat the virtual machines as if they are physical nodes (same level of care and concern and configuration attention to detail).

Best practices

Adhering to the best practices detailed on the "Hyper-V: Virtual Networking Survival Guide" (http://social.technet.microsoft.com/wiki/contents/articles/151.hyper-v-virtual-networking-survival-guide.aspx) goes a long way for starters. These may change over time but the current best practices are summarized here:

- Configure at least two physical NICs per virtual host. If additional load must be sustained, add additional physical network adapters as needed. Keep in mind both bandwidth *and* redundancy considerations.

- If separate communication is needed between the virtual machines and the physical server machines while maintaining communication with an external network, use an external virtual switch without a virtual network adapter in the management OS. This may be needed for backups of applications inside the virtual machine, where the host and guest can utilize the transfer speeds of the virtual bus.

- If two internal or private virtual networks are created in Hyper-V and two virtual machines are created on a separate IP subnet, they cannot communicate with each other. The virtual switch operates at layer 2 of the ISO/OSI Network Model. To achieve routing at higher levels, a router needs to be used, the same as would be done in a physical environment. Microsoft Routing and Remote Access Service (RRAS) may be used to achieve this functionality.

- When using an internal virtual network, create an exception to enable the virtual machines to communicate with the physical server in the firewall interface. By default, the Windows Firewall will prevent communication from the private network hosts. So simply create a firewall exception in the Firewall Control Panel applet or Windows Firewall with Advanced Security (wf.msc).
- When using virtual machines to communicate with the management OS on an internal virtual switch, ensure that they are on the same IP subnet.
- If the virtual machine experiences high traffic volume, it is recommended that a dedicated physical network adapter be assigned to the virtual machine.
- When possible, use Microsoft Windows Server 2012 NIC Teaming and use the teamed network adaptors to create Hyper-V virtual switches.
- If any 10GbE network adaptors are being used, make sure to utilize Windows Server 2012 Quality of Service (QoS) policies to restrict usage for different types of traffic, for example live migration, cluster shared volumes (CSV), and such.

VLAN concepts and troubleshooting

VLAN tagging is one of the often misunderstood technologies, so we'll spend some time briefly discussing it. The 802.1Q specification dictates that the VLAN ID tag is encapsulated within the Ethernet frame. This is why multiple virtual machines using the same physical NIC can communicate on different VLANs simultaneously. The physical NICs on the host machine must support VLAN tagging, and this feature must be enabled in the NIC properties on the host machine.

> **NOTE** All the VLAN IDs need to be trunked on the physical switch port connected to that Hyper-V host, otherwise there won't be any external connectivity.

Once this is set, all additional configuration is performed at the guest properties sheet in the Hyper-V administration console in the network adapter properties for the attached virtual NIC or the properties of the Virtual Network Switch. The VLAN tag has little to do with physical NIC interfaces and everything to do with the Ethernet packets transmitted from the host OS networking stack.

Only one VLAN ID can be configured on each virtual switch port, and it will be the one used by the virtual host. Likewise, each guest NIC assigned to it can have one VLAN assigned to it, so the maximum number of VLANs available to a Hyper-V virtual guest in Windows Server 2012 is 12.

Troubleshooting a VLAN network is just like troubleshooting any other network, with just another layer to remember in terms of connectivity. A VLAN delineates a virtual layer 2 isolation boundary. If a server is on VLAN 12 and another is on VLAN 15, even if they share the same subnet, they aren't going to talk since at the layer 2 level of the OSI model they can't see each other.

Windows PowerShell is available to query VLAN information in Windows Server 2012:

Get-VMNetworkAdapterVlan

Gets the virtual LAN settings configured on a virtual network adapter.

You can also use set VLAN information using this cmdlet:

Set-VMNetworkAdapterVlan

Configures the virtual LAN settings for the traffic through a virtual network adapter.

MAC addresses and virtual guests

By default Hyper-V has a MAC address range defined for 256 virtual guests. Hyper-V generates the MAC address as described below (mapping MAC address to aa-bb-cc-dd-ee-ff):

- The first three octets (aa-bb-cc) are Microsoft's IEEE organizationally Unique Identifier, 00:15:5D (which is common on all Hyper-V hosts).
- The next two octets (dd-ee) are derived from the last two octets of the server's IP address.
- The last octet (ff) is automatically generated from the range 0x0-0xFF.

Because the last octet is an 8-bit value, there is a default limit of 256 possible MAC addresses. After this amount is exceeded, guests that start up get this error:

The application encountered an error while attempting to change the state of '<Virtual machine name>'
Synthetic Ethernet Port (Instance ID CCE417C5-BDD9-4216-85CA-248620EE75C6): Failed to power on with Error 'Attempt to access invalid address'.

This is documented clearly in support article KB 2804678, which can be found at http://support.microsoft.com/kb/2804678. Remediation steps as of this writing are as follows:

1. Turn off the virtual machine, allocate a static MAC address that does not belong to the Hyper-V dynamic MAC address range, and then restart the virtual machine.
2. Increase the range of MAC addresses by modifying the fifth and/or the sixth octet of the default dynamic MAC address range.

You can set MAC addresses manually quite easily; it's in the GUI for the virtual NIC of each guest:

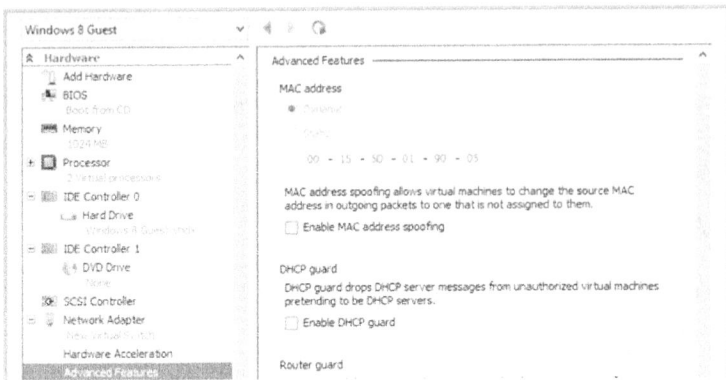

Network card drivers

There are some features virtual guests can utilize to optimize network traffic from the virtual guest network stack to the physical network card. These features are enabled by default:

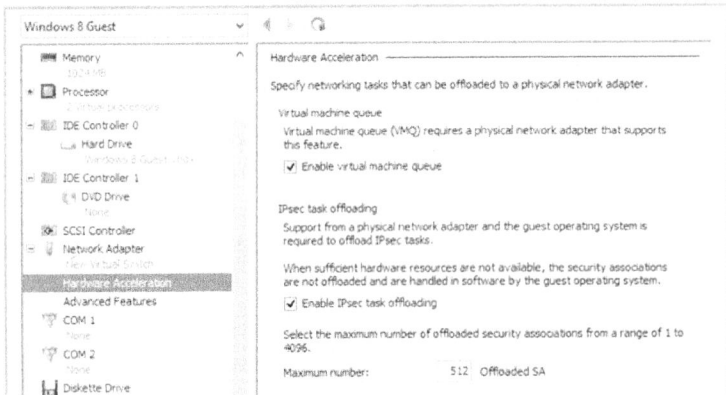

Please note that hardware acceleration features are entirely dependent on NIC driver implementation, and you may have support issues due to poorly written or out-of-date drivers. It is generally a best practice to keep drivers and firmware up to date to resolve this issue. If you run into poor performance and it gets better by disabling these feature sets, the next troubleshooting step should be to update the firmware and/or drivers of the NICs in use.

Example: Intel Teaming NIC driver and VMQ

Recently I encountered a problem with the Intel Teaming NIC driver and VMQ (or VMQd as Intel references it). Intel Teaming Software doesn't actually support this feature in virtual guests, and enabling it will cause random blue screens.

This issue is further documented at http://www.intel.com/support/network/sb/CS-030993.htm and http://www.aidanfinn.com/?p=10340.

—*Jeff Stokes, Senior Premier Field Engineer*

Additional resources

Here are a few additional resources concerning this topic:

- Hyper-V: Virtual Networking Survival Guide (TechNet Wiki) at: http://social.technet.microsoft.com/wiki/contents/articles/151.hyper-v-virtual-networking-survival-guide.aspx
- Windows Server 2012 Hyper-V Networking Evolved (TechNet Video) at: http://technet.microsoft.com/en-us/video/tdbe13-windows-server-2012-hyper-v-networking-evolved.aspx

Monitoring network performance

To truly know whether you've managed to optimize networking for Hyper-V hosts and the virtual machines running on them, you need to compare their performance before and after the configuration changes you've made to them. The inbox tool for doing this on the Windows Server platform is Performance Monitor.

In this section Thomas Roettinger, a Program Manager in the Partner and Customer Ecosystem Team at Microsoft, reviews how to use this tool and summarizes some key performance counters that you might want to consider monitoring. He also walks us through an example of troubleshooting a networking problem that is resolved by enabling bandwidth management for a virtual machine running on a Hyper-V host.

Using Performance Monitor

Windows Server lets you splitting network traffic based on usage type for Hyper-V. In general, these types are management, live migration, cluster shared volume, redirected I/O, and the network used by the tenants.

To determine your network usage, it's highly recommend you capture at least 24 hours of data. This ensures a full business day is monitored. Best would be to pick different days across a week to create a baseline or detect time slices where available network bandwidth is limited.

For example, let's say that you have a VDI environment where virtual machines are booted via PXE and get their hard disk streamed. You can imagine that available bandwidth might be low every morning when users are connecting to their virtual machines because of the resulting boot storm.

The Windows operating system offers performance counters for nearly all different components. You can gather performance data from these counters by using WMI or Performance Monitor. In this section I will show you how to use Performance Monitor to capture performance data for all important network components and also present thresholds that will help you to understand if there is a potential problem.

To start Performance Monitor, simply type **perfmon** at the new Start screen:

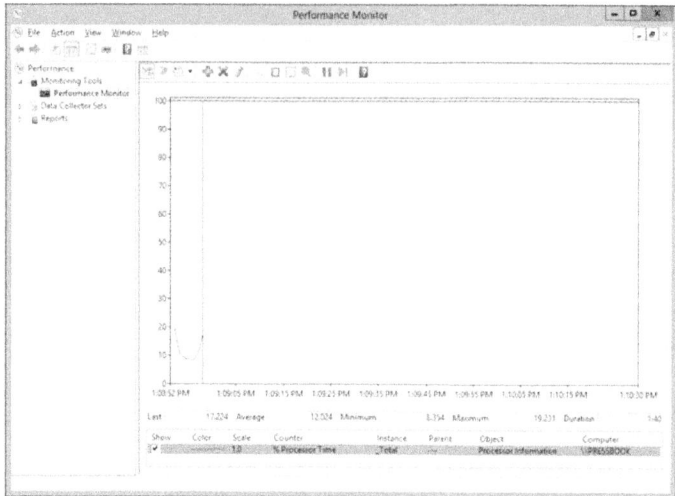

When you click Performance Monitor, you see a real-time view of your system. For capturing performance data over a longer period of time, you need to set up a data collector set. To do so expand Data Collector Sets, click User Defined, and right-click in the rightmost pane to create a new data collector set:

17

Specify a name for your data collector set and select Create Manually:

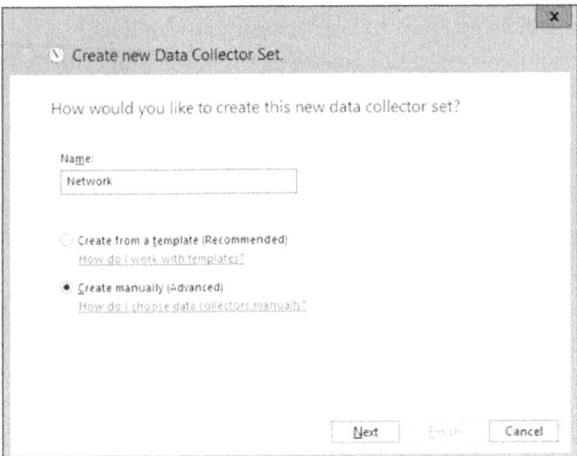

Next indicate that you want to include performance counters in that collector set by selecting Performance Counter under Create Data Logs:

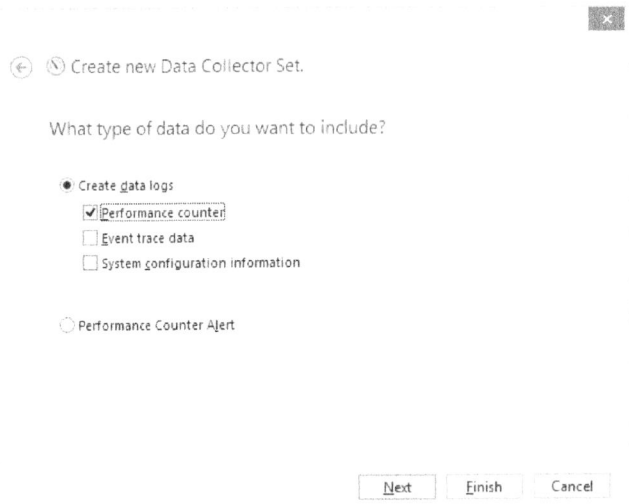

Next select the appropriate performance counters for networking. Walk through the following examples to understand the performance counters so that you can later use them in a data collector set:

Before we dive into the networking performance counters, you should know how to start and stop a data collector set and how to load and analyze data. Notice the green arrow and the stop symbol in the following screenshot. You could also use options in the data collector set properties to schedule the data collector set to run automatically:

To load a data collector set, go to Performance Monitor, right-click the Performance Monitor node, open Properties, and click the Source tab. There you can specify to load captured data from a log file.

When the file is loaded you also have the option to limit the data that is shown to a specific time window and to configure other properties:

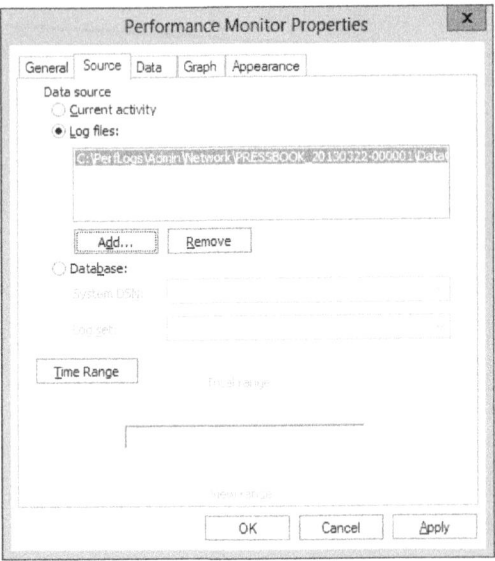

After the file is loaded you can add the counters you captured by clicking the green plus control and start investigating.

To make life easier, there is a tool called Performance Analysis of Logs (PAL) available at http://pal.codeplex.com. This tool contains a template with counters and thresholds for various Microsoft Windows Roles, as well as Exchange, SQL, and many others:

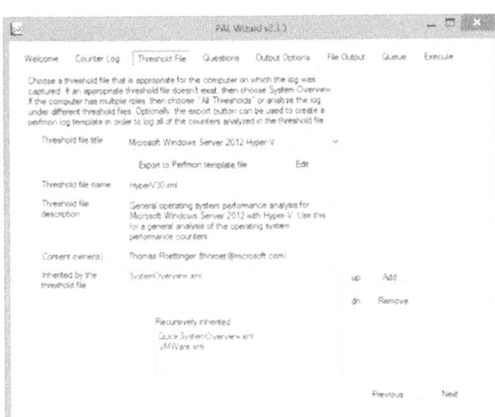

After exporting a template from PAL you can import it to a data collector set. The log file that you then get from the data collector set created from your performance data then needs to be imported into PAL. PAL then analyzes the log file and creates an HTML report with all the findings. Give it a try!

Network performance counters

The sections below summarize some key performance counters you can track for monitoring the following networking components:
- Physical network adapter
- Virtual network adapter
- Virtual switch

Physical network adapters

To monitor physical network adapters, use these performance counters:

- **Network Interface(*)\Bytes Received/sec** This counter measures the rate at which bytes have been received over each physical network adapter. Thresholds are more than 50 percent and more than 80 percent. Values depend upon the maximum available bandwidth, for example a 1-gigabit link allows 120,000,000 bytes/sec. Using this data, you can compute the percentage of utilization.

- **Network Interface(*)\Bytes Sent/sec** This counter measures the rate at which bytes have been sent over each physical network adapter. Thresholds are more than 50 percent and 80 percent. Values depend upon the maximum available bandwidth, for example a 1-gigabit link allows 120,000,000 bytes/sec. Using this data, you can compute the percentage of utilization.

- **Network Interface(*)\Current Bandwidth** This counter measures the available bandwidth per interface. If a network card is connected to a 1-gigabit switch port you should check that it is not switching to another port speed due to auto-sensing, for example.

- **Network Interface(*)\Output Queue Length** This counter measures the number of packets waiting in the output queue. Thresholds are more than 1 packet and more than 2 packets.

- **Network Interface(*)\Packets Outbound Errors** This counter measures the number of packets with outbound errors. The threshold is more than 1 packet.

- **Network Interface(*)\Packets Receive Errors** This counter measures the number of packets with receive errors. The threshold is more than 1 packet.

Virtual network adapters

To monitor virtual network adapters, use these performance counters:

- **Hyper-V Virtual Network Adapter(*)\Bytes/sec** This counter measures the total rate at which bytes have been received and sent over each virtual network adapter from each virtual machine. Thresholds are more than 50 percent and more than 80

21

percent. Values depend upon the maximum available bandwidth, for example a 1-gigabit link allows 120,000,000 bytes/sec. Using this data, you can compute the percentage of utilization. Remember that if you are not using QoS rules, it is possible for a single virtual machine to take up all the available bandwidth.

- **Hyper-V Virtual Network Adapter(*)\Bytes Received/sec** This counter measures the rate at which bytes have been received over each virtual network adapter from each virtual machine. Thresholds are more than 50 percent and more than 80 percent. Values depend upon the maximum available bandwidth, for example a 1-gigabit link allows 120,000,000 bytes/sec. Using this data, you can compute the percentage of utilization. Remember that if you are not using QoS rules, it is possible for a single virtual machine to take up all the available bandwidth.

- **Hyper-V Virtual Network Adapter(*)\Bytes Sent/sec** This counter measures the rate at which bytes have been sent over each virtual network adapter from each virtual machine. Thresholds are more than 50 percent and more than 80 percent. Values depend upon the maximum available bandwidth, for example a 1-gigabit link allows 120,000,000 bytes/sec. Using this data, you can compute the percentage of utilization. Remember that if you are not using QoS rules, it is possible for a single virtual machine to take up all the available bandwidth.

Virtual switch

To monitor the Hyper-V virtual switch, use these performance counters:

- **\Hyper-V Virtual Switch(*)\Bytes/sec** This counter measures the total number of bytes per second traversing the virtual switch. You'll also want to look at the sent and received bytes per second for each port where a virtual machine is connected.

- **\Hyper-V Virtual Switch Port(*)\Bytes Received/sec** This counter measures the total number of bytes per second received for a given switch port that belongs to a virtual machine. If two virtual machines are on the same host, just the first packet leaves the host to determine the shortest path.

- **\Hyper-V Virtual Switch Port(*)\Bytes Sent/sec** This counter measures the total number of bytes per second sent for a given switch port that belongs to a virtual machine. If two virtual machines are on the same host, just the first packet leaves the host to determine the shortest path.

- **\Hyper-V Virtual Switch Processor(*)\Number of VMQs** This counter measures the number of VMQs targeting the virtual switch processor. The number of queues depends on the network card. Each network card that is VMQ capable provides a limited number of queues.

Example: Exhausted bandwidth

Patricia is an administrator who works for a hoster. The hoster is using a shared fabric for the tenants. She gets a call from the help desk informing her that some customers are having problems accessing their servers and that connections are getting dropped.

After looking up the customers, she finds out that all the customers having issues are sharing the same Hyper-V host.

> **NOTE** This also could have been an issue where access to a particular service is slow or impossible in an enterprise environment.

Patricia logs on to that Hyper-V host and opens Performance Monitor. She uses the real-time monitoring view and adds the performance counter for the physical network card. She uses the counters shown in the following screenshot:

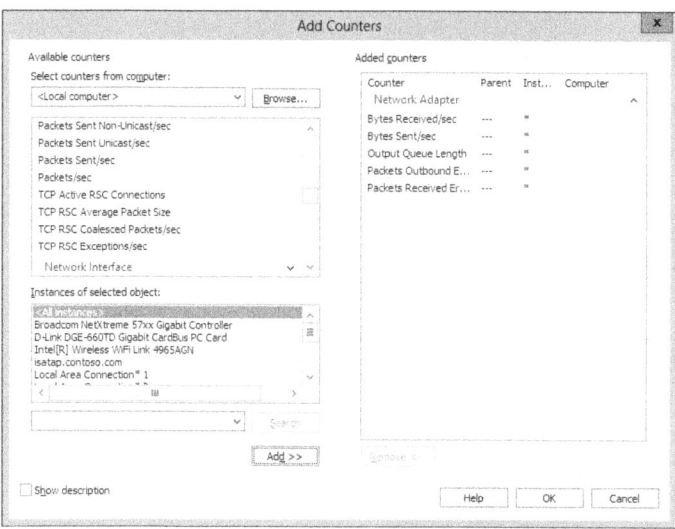

This Hyper-V host has a dedicated network adapter that is used by the tenants. As shown in the screenshot, the physical network card that is used for the tenant switch is a Broadcom NetXtreme 57xx Gigabit Controller. The following Windows PowerShell cmdlet can be used to determine this:

Get-VMSwitch

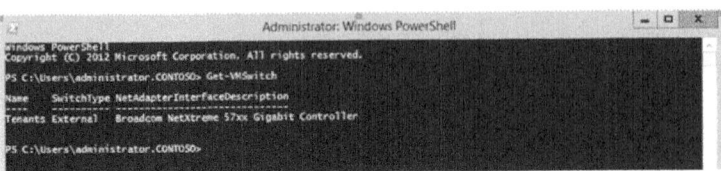

The bytes received/sec for the Broadcom NetXtreme 57xx Gigabit Controller show a value of 100,850,637 bytes/sec (101 MB/sec) for incoming traffic (received bytes/sec). To calculate the network utilization, Patricia divides 101 by 1.2 (1 percent of 1 gigabit), which results in 84 percent:

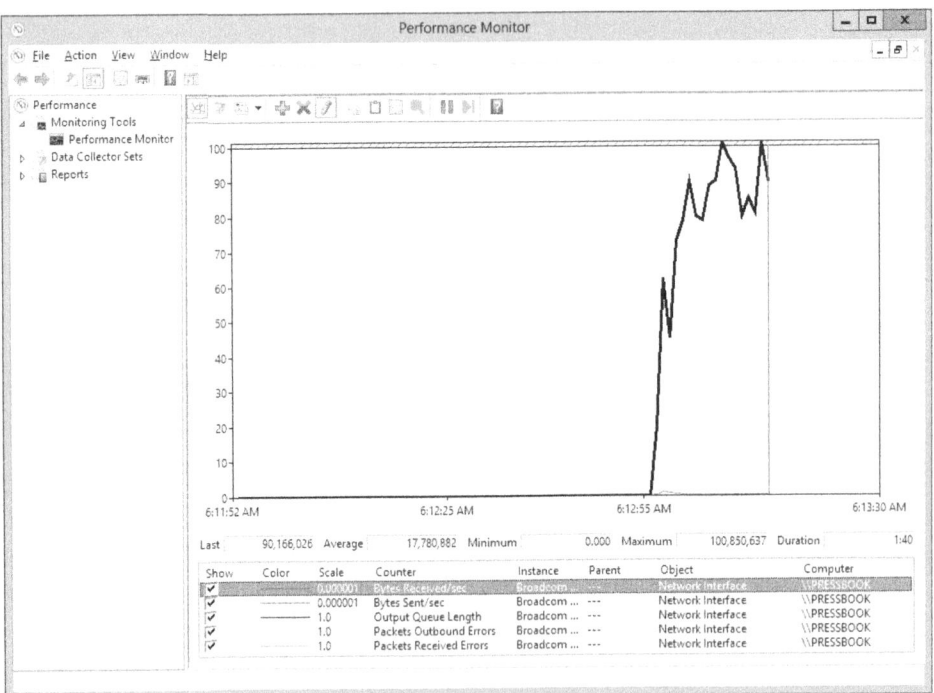

Next, Patricia must identify which tenant virtual machine is consuming all the bandwidth. She removes all the previous counters for the physical network adapter. She then adds the received bytes/sec counter for each virtual machine network adapter:

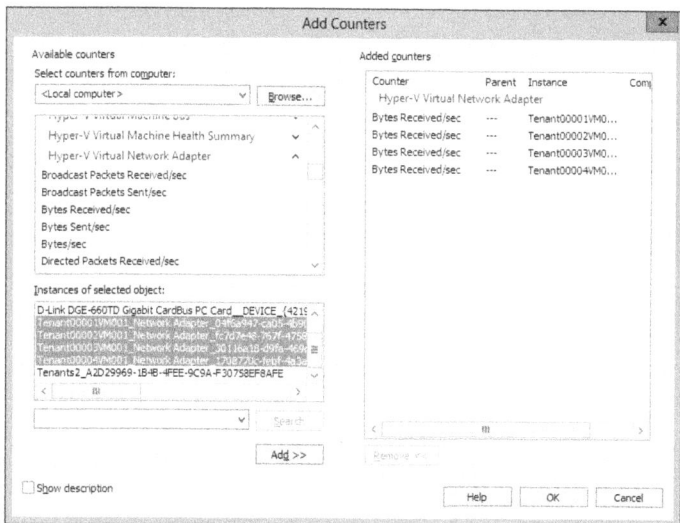

She detects that the "Tenant00001VM001" virtual network adapter has a value of 85,879,656 bytes/sec (86 MB/sec). This tenant virtual machine is using 71 percent of total available bandwidth of 1 gigabit:

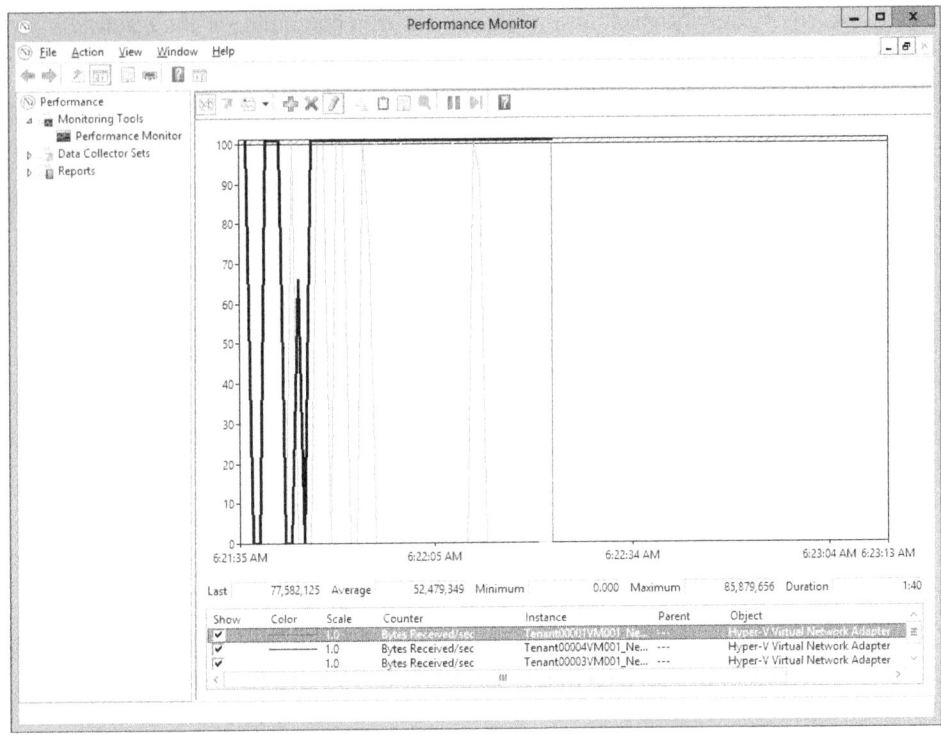

Patricia evaluates the virtual machine settings for the virtual network adapter and detects that no network QoS rule is configured for it. She enables bandwidth management and caps the bandwidth at a maximum of 200 MB/sec:

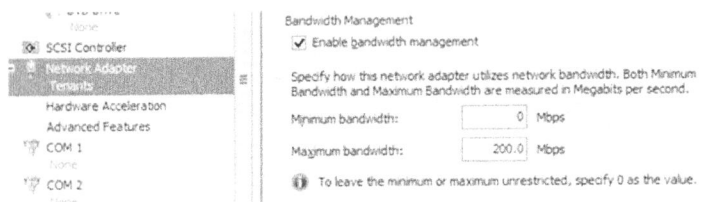

Instead of capping the network bandwidth, Patricia could have configured a minimum bandwidth for each virtual machine.

—*Thomas Roettinger, Program Manager, Partner and Customer Ecosystem Team*

Additional resources

Here is an additional resource concerning this topic:

- Windows Performance Monitor (TechNet Library) at: http://technet.microsoft.com/en-us/library/cc749249.aspx

Virtual switch

The Hyper-V virtual switch in Windows Server 2012 has new capabilities that can provide for tenant isolation, traffic shaping, protection against malicious virtual machines, and easier troubleshooting of issues. The virtual switch is also extensible and is built on an open platform that enables independent software vendors to add or extend the capabilities provided natively in the virtual switch. Non-Microsoft extensions can be developed that can emulate the full capabilities of hardware-based switches to allow for implementing more complex virtual environments and solutions.

The virtual switch is implemented as a layer 2 virtual network that you can use to connect virtual machines to the physical network. The virtual switch also provides policy enforcement for security, isolation, and service levels and supports Network Device Interface Specification (NDIS) filter drivers and Windows Filtering Platform (WFP) callout drivers to support non-Microsoft extensible plug-ins that can provide enhanced networking and security capabilities.

In this section, Madhan Sivakumar, a Software Development Engineer II on the Windows Core Networking team at Microsoft, explains how you can reduce network downtime using the rich diagnostics available for the Windows Server 2012 Hyper-V virtual switch.

Reducing network downtime with rich diagnostics in Hyper-V virtual switch

Imagine a situation where you have just deployed hundreds of virtual machines across different hosts and now you are getting reports that some virtual machines have lost network connectivity. This situation is not hard to imagine for most IT/network administrators since most have had to deal with this issue at some point in the past.

There could be many reasons for broken network connectivity; for example, misconfiguration, wrong placement of virtual machines, miscommunication between the network administrator and virtual machine administrator. What the administrator dreads the most is the downtime caused by broken connectivity as they wait for the support team to diagnose the issue and restore connectivity. Reducing network downtime was one of the highest priorities in developing Windows Server 2012, which gives administrators a rich set of diagnostics tools and features to quickly identify issues and fix them. This section goes over these new features and some improvements made to existing features.

System event log

When you receive an issue report, the first thing you do is look at the system event log. There are a number of error/warning events in the system event log that are logged by the provider Hyper-V vmswitch, which captures the configuration/setup errors with enough detail to help you understand the issue. Let's say you start with the system event log to diagnose virtual machine network connectivity issues and notice the following error event being logged. You'll know that virtual machine connectivity has been blocked because one of the required extensions is missing:

Connectivity has been blocked for NIC 32FC2EED-6AA4-4F03-8926-3C5AF80EF5A6--A610DE2F-0B59-40B1-91C1-AB513E0F5F6E (Friendly Name: Network Adapter) on port 83805C62-C57F-4EC1-B000-433D1914A16C (Friendly Name:). Extension {5cbf81be-5055-47cd-9055-a76b2b4e369e} is required on the port, but it is not active on switch EF4EE212-5D11-477C-BE86-B131ECA4E397 (Friendly Name: ext).

You can make use of the new PowerShell cmdlets to get the list of switch extensions currently installed:

PS C:\test> Get-VMSwitchExtension ext

```
Id                  : 5CBF81BE-5055-47CD-9055-A76B2B4E369E
Name                : Switch Extensibility Test Extension 2
Vendor              : Microsoft
Version             : 6.0.5019.0
ExtensionType       : Filter
ParentExtensionId   :
ParentExtensionName :
SwitchId            : EF4EE212-5D11-477C-BE86-B131ECA4E397
SwitchName          : ext
Enabled             : False
Running             : False
ComputerName        : 27-3145J0630
IsDeleted           : False
```

Here you notice that the extension with ID 5CBF81BE-5055-47CD-9055-A76B2B4E369E from the event log is not enabled on this switch even though it is marked as mandatory for the virtual machine. Enabling this extension from PowerShell will restore network connectivity to the virtual machine.

As you can see, Windows Server 2012 logs these events with as much detail as possible so that it is easy for administrators to figure out what is going on. From this particular event log, the administrator knows which virtual machine (from the NIC and port names/friendly names) connected to which switch has connectivity issues, along with the reason for broken connectivity. This is just one example of more than 50 events that are logged to the system log by vmswitch for easy diagnosis.

Performance counters

In the above scenario, connectivity is restored to the virtual machine after the required extension network is installed. However, imagine you discover that two virtual machines connected to the same virtual switch are unable to connect to each other. If you are unable to find sufficient information in the system event log to diagnose this issue, the next step would be to launch Performance Monitor and take a look at the following counter providers:

- Hyper-V Virtual Switch
- Hyper-V Virtual Switch Port
- Hyper-V Virtual Network Adapter

For diagnosing network connectivity issues, the following counters would be of interest:

- Dropped Packets Incoming/sec
- Dropped Packets Outgoing/sec
- Extensions Dropped Packets Incoming/sec
- Extension Dropped Packets Outgoing/sec

Separate counters clearly identify where the packets are being dropped: switch or switch extensions. When you see that the Dropped Packets Incoming/sec is high, you know that there has been some misconfiguration in the switch:

In the above example, the parent partition is unable to communicate with the virtual machine named VM1. The dropped counters of the parent partition virtual NIC is zero. However, the outgoing dropped counter of the virtual machine virtual network adapter is greater than zero. If all of the virtual NIC and switch dropped counters show zero dropped packets, it would be a good idea to examine whether the packet is getting dropped in the virtual machine itself by checking the firewall and other settings in the virtual machine OS.

Diagnostic event log and packet capture

Now, you have identified the switch is dropping outgoing packets from the virtual machine, but you don't yet know the reason. One way to determine the root cause would be to go over all the switch port configurations manually to check if you have missed something. However, this is tedious and time consuming. Since the goal is to minimize network downtime, a new Windows Server 2012 feature makes this process fast. You can use the diagnostic event log to capture Vmswitch debug events. Here is the command to start the debug channel:

Netsh trace start provider=Microsoft-Windows-Hyper-V-Vmswitch

After reproduciing the connectivity issue, stop the tracing session:

Netsh trace stop

You can open the generated ETL file using Event Viewer or Netmon (more on opening these files using Netmon later). As the packet flows through vmswitch, a number of events are being generated to trace the flow:

- When vmswitch receives the packet from the source NIC:

    NBL received from Nic CCF4C0A2-B213-4A35-80B2-4D97F4A6A46F (Friendly Name: TestLogicalSwitch) in switch 1C3F4C4C-47B9-4BE2-A563-F2800468D9B9 (Friendly Name: TestLogicalSwitch)

- When the packet is routed from the source NIC to the destination NIC(s):

    NBL routed from Nic CCF4C0A2-B213-4A35-80B2-4D97F4A6A46F (Friendly Name: TestLogicalSwitch) to Nic ABE31850-AE81-4DD7-BB48-7F7D51A04053--0 (Friendly Name: Legacy Network Adapter) on switch 1C3F4C4C-47B9-4BE2-A563-F28004

- When the packet is delivered to the destination NIC:

    NBL delivered to Nic ABE31850-AE81-4DD7-BB48-7F7D51A04053--0 (Friendly Name: Legacy Network Adapter) in switch 1C3F4C4C-47B9-4BE2-A563-F2800468D9B9 (Friendly Name: TestLogicalSwitch)

When packets are dropped in vmswitch for any reason, you'll usually see a corresponding dropped event log entry:

NBL originating from Nic ABE31850-AE81-4DD7-BB48-7F7D51A04053--0 (Friendly Name: Legacy Network Adapter) was dropped in switch 1C3F4C4C-47B9-4BE2-A563-F2800468D9B9 (Friendly Name: TestLogicalSwitch), Reason Failed Security Policy

For some dropped event logs, there would be another event log with more details. In the previous example, the packet was dropped because of a failed security policy, but it is unclear which security policy actually caused the drop. This event is followed by another event giving more details:

A packet was dropped on port 72542DDC-A517-4E70-8BB6-B33B7C409C1F (Friendly Name: Dynamic Ethernet Switch Port) on switch 1C3F4C4C-47B9-4BE2-A563-F2800468D9B9 (Friendly Name: TestLogicalSwitch) because the packet is filtered by Port ACL.

With this event, you can immediately identify why the virtual machines were unable to ping each other. These inter-virtual machine packets were dropped due to a Port ACL configured on one of the switch ports. You can identify the port where the packets were dropped by looking at the NIC/port dropped counters. At this point you just need to review the port ACLs that are set on this switch port to either fix this issue or verify that the packet was correctly dropped according to the rules.

Packet capture within vmswitch

One of the most common tools used for diagnosis is packet capture. Until the current release of Windows Server, you could not capture packets flowing within vmswitch. With the extensible virtual switch in Windows Server 2012, you can capture packets at both ingress (when the packet enters the switch) and egress (when the packet leaves the switch). This is done through the unified tracing packet capture driver, which in Windows 8 has been updated to a switch extension. To turn on capture within vmswitch, use the following command:

Netsh trace start provider=Microsoft-Windows-Hyper-V-Vmswitch capture=yes, capturetype=vmswitch

This will capture all packets flowing through all switches on the host. To include packet capture in the host NDIS stack, use the following:

capturetype=both

To stop the tracing session and generate an ETL file, use the following command:

Netsh trace stop

This ETL file can be opened using Netmon. You need the parsers to view this capture (and the vmswitch events mentioned in the earlier section) using Netmon. The parsers can be downloaded from the CodePlex site at http://nmparsers.codeplex.com/releases.

The following screenshot shows capture at ingress:

This looks like any other Netmon capture. This is an ICMP Reply packet. However, this capture has additional information that helps in quicker analysis. This also captures the VM Name, Port ID, Source NIC name, and so on. The capture at egress also includes these fields along with the destination information:

In the above egress capture, the packet is being routed from VM1 to an internal virtual NIC on the host. In the case of broadcast/multicast packets, the capture will show a destination array with information about each destination in the array.

I hope that these new features will help you diagnose issues faster and more easily, thereby reducing the network downtime for virtual machines and the host.

—*Madhan Sivakumar, Software Development Engineer II, Windows Core Networking*

Additional resources

Here are a few additional resources concerning this topic:

- Hyper-V Virtual Switch Overview (TechNet Library) at: http://technet.microsoft.com/en-us/library/hh831823.aspx
- Hyper-V: Virtual Networking Survival Guide (TechNet Wiki) at: http://social.technet.microsoft.com/wiki/contents/articles/151.hyper-v-virtual-networking-survival-guide.aspx
- Hyper-V Access Control Lists (ACLs) (TechNet Library) at: http://technet.microsoft.com/en-us/library/jj679878.aspx#bkmk_portacls

Port mirroring

Port mirroring is a new capability built into the Hyper-V virtual switch in Windows Server 2012. With port mirroring, traffic sent to or from a Hyper-V virtual switch port is copied and sent to a mirror port.

Port mirroring supports a wide range of different applications and uses. An entire ecosystem of network visibility companies exist that have created products designed to consume port mirror data for performance management, security analysis, and network diagnostics. With Hyper-V virtual switch port mirroring, you can now select the switch ports that are monitored as well as the switch port that receives copies of all the traffic. Combined with either the Windows PowerShell support included in Windows Server 2012 or with third-party applications, port mirroring can be a useful tool for troubleshooting a wide range of Hyper-V networking problems.

In this section, Thomas Roettinger, a Program Manager with the Partner and Customer Ecosystem Team at Microsoft, walks through a basic demonstration of how to use port mirroring.

Port mirroring example

Port Mirroring was introduced in Windows Server 2012 Hyper-V. This feature copies traffic sent to and from a virtual switch port to a mirror port. This feature is useful in many different scenarios, including troubleshooting network-related issues.

In the following example, all traffic sent to and from virtual machine "Tenant1" gets copied to another virtual machine called "Sniffer." The Sniffer virtual machine has Microsoft Network Monitor installed.

Patricia is an administrator who needs to mirror traffic of a virtual machine for the network team. She opens the virtual machine settings for the source virtual machine called Tenant1. Under Network Adapter, she clicks Advanced Features, and then she selects Source as the mirroring mode in the Port Mirroring section:

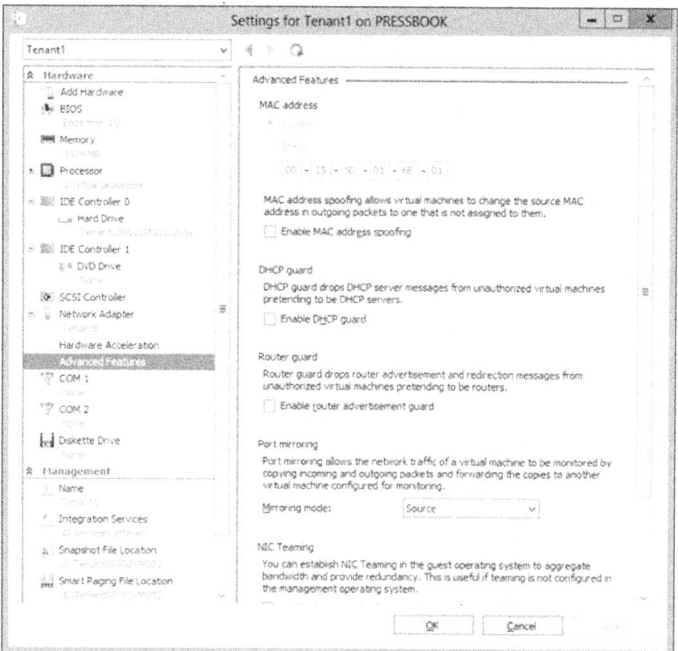

The virtual machine used by the network team is called Sniffer. Patricia opens the virtual machine settings for Sniffer and configures the port mirroring mode as Destination in Advanced Features of the Network Adapter:

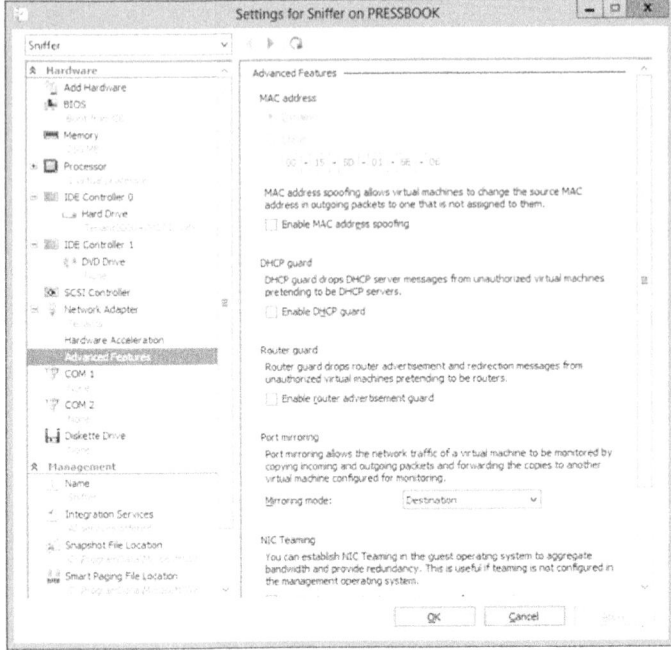

To achieve the same configuration via PowerShell, she could run the following commands:

On the source machine:

Set-VMNetworkAdapter –VMName Tenant1 –PortMirroring Source

On the destination machine:

Set-VMNetworkAdapter –VMName Sniffer –PortMirroring Destination

Patricia installs Microsoft Network Monitor inside Sniffer. To capture all, she must enable traffic P-Mode (Promiscuous Mode) in Microsoft Network Monitor:

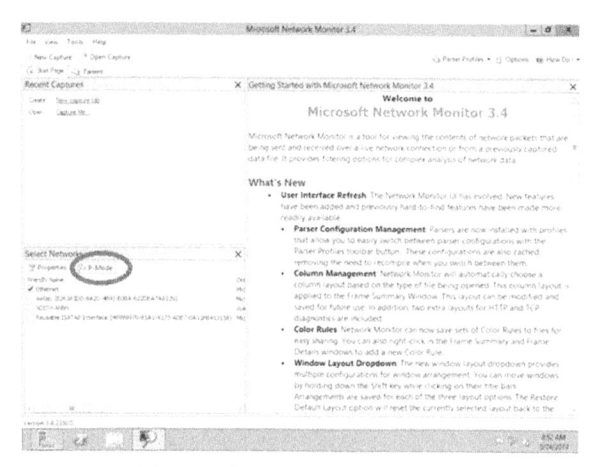

For a quick test, she pings Tenant1 from a third machine called DC01. As she captures traffic with the virtual machine Sniffer, she can see the ICMP traffic from DC01 to 192.168.0.205, which belongs to Tenant1:

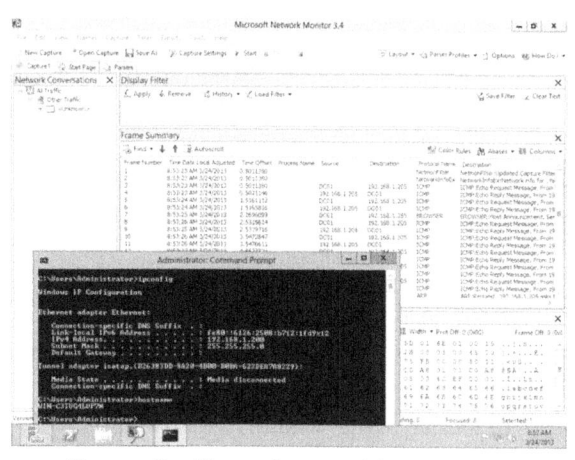

—Thomas Roettinger, Program Manager, Partner and Customer Ecosystem Team

Additional resources

Here are a few additional resources concerning this topic:

- What's New in Hyper-V Virtual Switch (TechNet Library) at:
  http://technet.microsoft.com/en-us/library/jj679878.aspx
- Packet Flow through the Extensible Switch Data Path (Windows Dev Center - Hardware) at:
  http://msdn.microsoft.com/en-us/library/windows/hardware/hh582269(v=vs.85).aspx

MAC addresses

With Hyper-V you can use Virtual Network Manager to specify a range of media access control (MAC) addresses to assign to virtual machines and to constrain the range of dynamic MAC addresses available. When multiple Hyper-V hosts use the same subnet, however, you need to avoid duplicating the same address range on more than one host to prevent potential conflicts that would result if the same MAC address is assigned to more than one virtual machine on the subnet.

In this section, Thomas Roettinger, a Program Manager with the Partner and Customer Ecosystem Team at Microsoft, demonstrates how to troubleshoot several issues associated with duplicate MAC addresses in Hyper-V environments.

Hyper-V and MAC addresses

When you install the Hyper-V role, a MAC address range is created. When you look at the MAC address, it is simple to understand where the bytes come from:

- **00-15-5D** Microsoft IEEE Organizationally Unique Identifier
- **01-66** These two bytes come from the first IPv4 Address of the host. The two lowest octets are convert hex. 01-66 maps to 1.102, so in this case the IP was 192.168.1.102.
- **00** The last byte is 00 for minimum and FF for the maximum.

In this example, the MAC address range is:

- **00-15-5D-01-66-00** Minimum MAC address
- **00-15-5D-01-66-FF** Maximum MAC address

You can evaluate your MAC address range by looking at the Windows Registry:

Computer\HKEY_LOCAL_MACHINE\SOFTWARE\Microsoft\Windows NT\Current Version\Virtualization

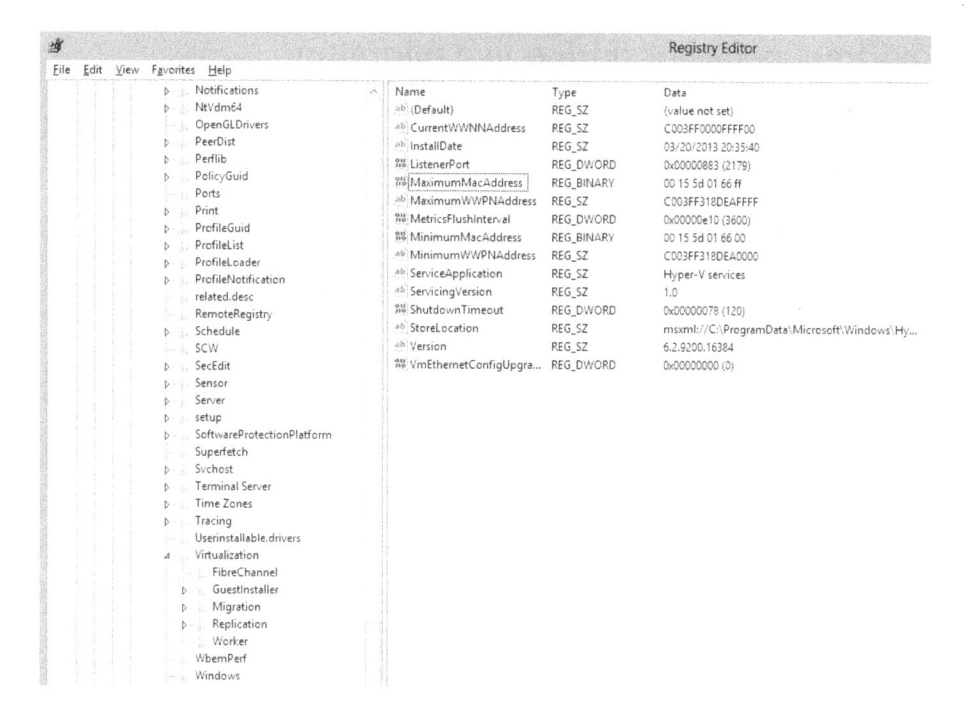

Duplicate MAC addresses

After you understand the basics, it's time to learn how two or more virtual machines can have the identical MAC address. This can happen in the following scenarios:

1. A Hyper-V host has more than 255 virtual machines, which means the pool is depleted. If one or more virtual machines are stopped or in saved state and a new virtual machine is created, one of those MAC addresses will be reused.

2. During installation, a Hyper-V host is assigned the same first IP address that another host was assigned during installation. This results in the same MAC address range.

3. Cloning a Hyper-V host for deployment will include the MAC address range in the registry. This results in a MAC address range overlapping across multiple hosts. Since Windows Server 2008 R2 Hyper-V is sysprep aware.

NOTE Hyper-V detects duplicate MAC addresses and prevents virtual machines from starting. This detection mechanism works for a single Hyper-V host.

The Microsoft management tool System Center Virtual Machine Manager solves these problems by using bare metal deployment and maintaining a global MAC address database for all virtual machines.

MAC address behavior during live migration

What happens to the MAC address when a virtual machine is moved between hosts with live migration? During a live migration the MAC address will not change, but after a reboot of the virtual machine, it will be assigned a new MAC address from the destination host MAC pool. A virtual machine running a Linux distribution requires a static MAC address before moving it with live or quick migration to another host without losing the network connection.

The following is an example of a virtual machine that is live migrated.

The source host has the following MAC address range:

- **00-15-5D-01-66-00** Minimum MAC address
- **00-15-5D-01-66-FF** Maximum MAC address

The destination host has the following MAC address range:

- **00-15-5D-01-6E-00** Minimum MAC address
- **00-15-5D-01-6E-FF** Maximum MAC address

Here is the MAC address before the live migration:

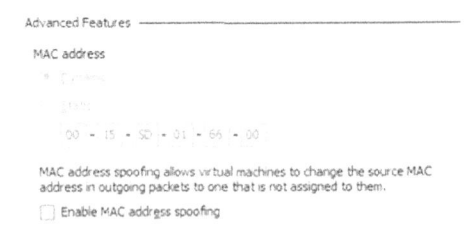

And here is the MAC address after the live migration:

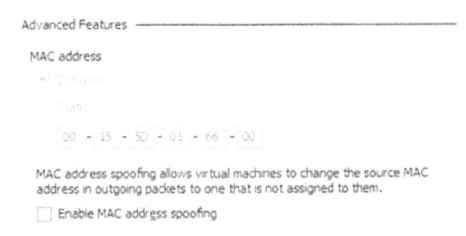

Here is the MAC address after first reboot on the destination host:

NOTE When you have an application running inside a virtual machine that has its licensing tied to the MAC address be aware that this kind of change might have some effect upon how the application functions.

Duplicate MAC addresses on a standalone host

If you have a Hyper-V host with 255 virtual machines actively running, the MAC address pool is depleted.

Patricia is an administrator who creates an additional machine called duplicated MAC. When she tries to start that virtual machine she receives the following error message:

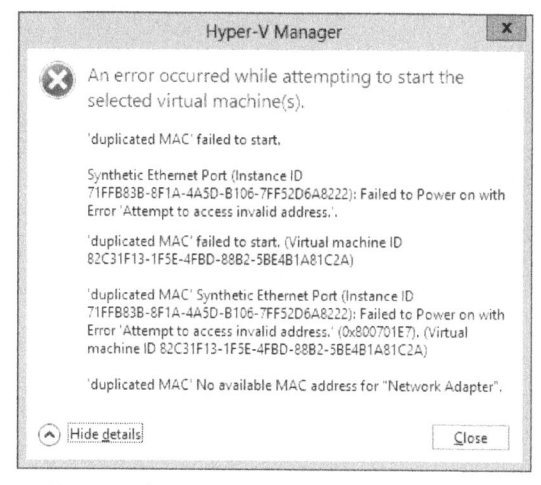

Hyper-V detects that no additional MAC address is available in the pool and prevents the start.

Patricia puts one of the virtual machines into saved state, and she's able to successfully start the virtual machine duplicated MAC. However, Hyper-V also prevents Patricia from resuming the virtual machine that she previously put in saved state.

To determine which other virtual machine is causing this problem, Patricia can run the following PowerShell command to generate a list of all the virtual machines and their assigned MAC addresses:

Get-VM|Get-VMNetworkAdapter | ft vmname,macaddress

Duplicated MAC addresses due to address range overlapping

Patricia is facing a problem with a virtual machine. When she pings the target, it responds only periodically.

To check for duplicate MAC addresses across all Hyper-V hosts, Patricia runs the following PowerShell script:

```
$HyperVHosts = @("host1","host2")
foreach ($HyperVServer in $HyperVHosts)
{
Get-VM –Computername $HyperVServer |get-vmnetadapter|ft vmname,macaddress,computername
}
```

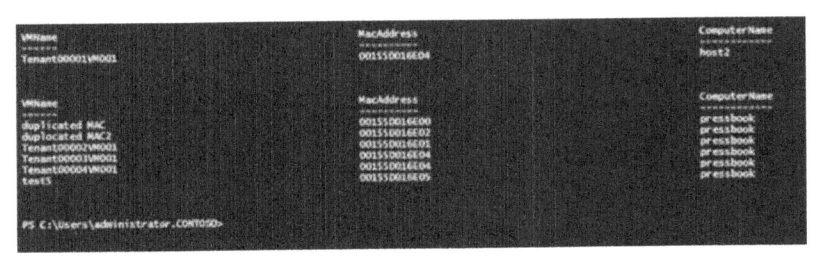

The output indicates that the two Hyper-V hosts have the same MAC address range. To verify, Patricia needs to validate the values for minimum and maximum MAC address on both hosts. The values are stored in the following registry hive:

Computer\HKEY_LOCAL_MACHINE\SOFTWARE\Microsoft\Windows NT\Current Version\Virtualization

—*Thomas Roettinger, Program Manager, Partner and Customer Ecosystem Team*

Additional resources

Here are a few additional resources concerning this topic:

- What's New in Hyper-V Virtual Switch (TechNet Library) at: http://technet.microsoft.com/en-us/library/jj679878.aspx
- Hyper-V: MAC address allocation and apparent network issues MAC collisions can cause (John Howard's blog) at: http://blogs.technet.com/b/jhoward/archive/2008/07/15/hyper-v-mac-address-allocation-and-apparent-network-issues-mac-collisions-can-cause.aspx

Single Root I/O Virtualization

Single Root I/O Virtualization (SR-IOV) is a standard developed by the Peripheral Component Interconnect Special Interest Group (PCI-SIG) that works in conjunction with system chipset support for virtualization technologies. SR-IOV enables network traffic to bypass the software switch layer of the Hyper-V virtualization stack to allow SR-IOV–capable devices to be assigned directly to a virtual machine. It does this by providing remapping of interrupts and DMA.

Hyper-V in Windows Server 2012 includes built-in support for SR-IOV–capable network devices to allow an SR-IOV virtual function of a physical network adapter to be assigned directly to a virtual machine. This increases network throughput and reduces network latency for virtual machines running on Hyper-V hosts while also reducing the host CPU overhead required for processing network traffic.

In this section, Keith Hill, a Senior Support Escalation Engineer with the Windows Server Core High Availability Team, digs deeper into what SR-IOV is and how it works, and he also walks us through a troubleshooting example.

SR-IOV Overview

One of the new features included with Hyper-V in Windows Server 2012 is Single Root I/O Virtualization (SR-IOV). SR-IOV is a specification that was created by Peripheral Component Interconnect Special Interest Group (PCI-SIG) in 2010. SR-IOV allows a PCIe device to appear to be multiple separate physical PCIe devices.

> **NOTE** The SR-IOV standard can be downloaded from http://www.pcisig.com/specifications/iov/single_root/ (PCI-SIG membership required).

It is important to note that the SR-IOV standard applies to all PCIe devices, including storage. However with Windows Server 2012, Microsoft looked where the biggest gains would be in using SR-IOV. Microsoft decided to exclusively work on SR-IOV for networking as the only supported device.

Windows Server 2008 R2 has two types of virtual network cards: the emulated network adapter (Legacy Network Adapter) and the synthetic network adapter (Network Adapter). I think that most of us know why one shouldn't use an emulated network card over a software network card. But because understanding this is important to the topic of this chapter, I will briefly go over it here..

The emulated network card is the worst performing of the two and should be used to PXE boot a virtual machine. The software NIC is the default and gains a performance boost because of the VMBus, an in-memory pipeline, which forwards the device request to the parent partition and then to the physical device. But there is overhead associated with the I/O path with the software NIC.

In short, software devices introduce latency, increase overall path length, and consume compute cycles. With higher network speeds and the number of supported virtual machines on a system it would not be uncommon to see a single core being consumed by 5 to 7 Gbps of network traffic that is generated by the virtual machines running on Windows Server 2008 R2 SP1.

So that led Microsoft to offer other alternatives for those scenarios. All welcome the arrival of SR-IOV in Windows Server 2012. This is a secure device model, well relative to the software-based device-sharing I/O that has lower latency, higher throughput, and lower compute overhead. It offers all of this plus it scales well as the number of virtual machines increase.

How SR-IOV works

So how does SR-IOV work? In Windows Server 2012 Hyper-V, SR-IOV works through physical functions (PF) and virtual functions (VF).

PFs are PCIe functions of a network adapter that supports the SR-IOV specification. The PF includes all of the extended capabilities in the PCIe base specifications. This capability is used to configure and manage the SR-IOV functionality of the network adapter, including enabling virtualization and exposing the VFs. VFs are lightweight functions that lack the configuration resources. Each VF shares one or more physical resources on the network adapter.

For example, the VF shares the external network port with the PF and other VFs. While VFs are transient, keep in mind that the PFs are always available (that is, if the PCIe device is not disabled). It is important to understand that a VF cannot exist without a PF. For illustration purposes, let's take a look at the software components in the following diagram:

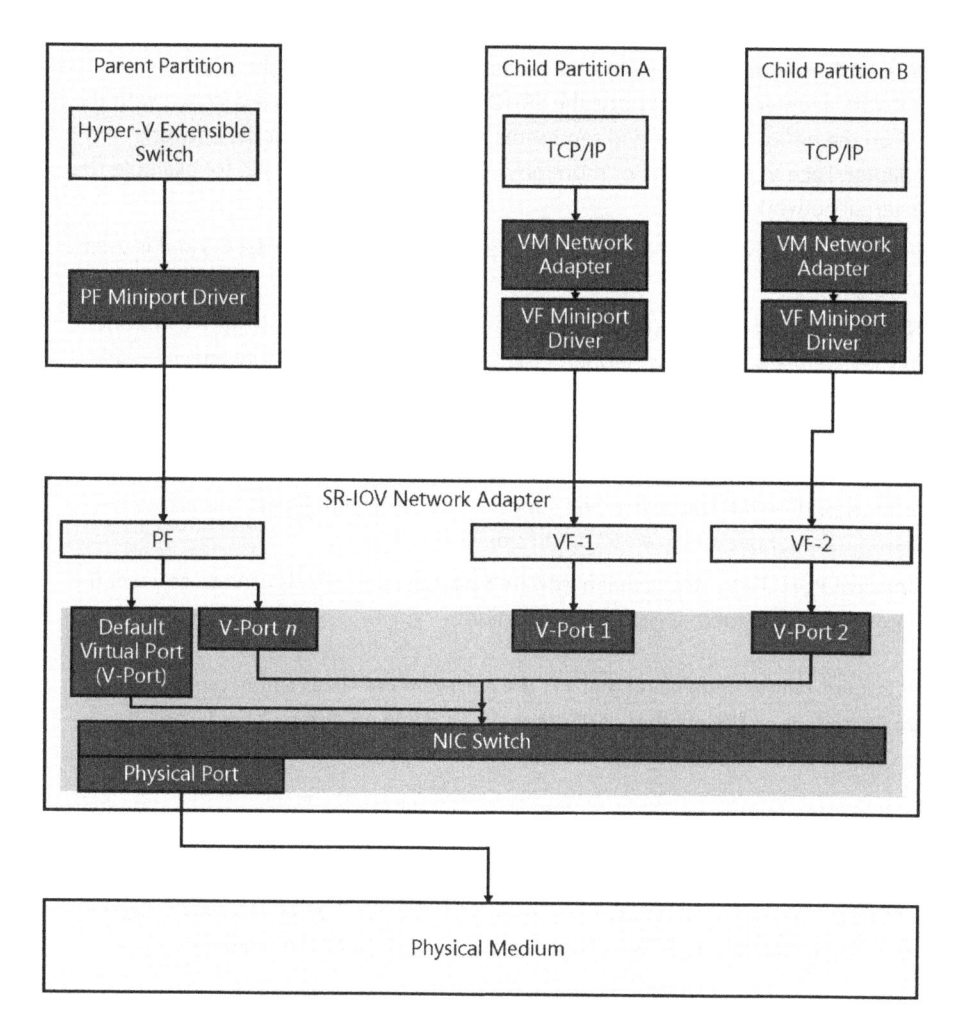

NOTE Hyper-V child partitions are also known as virtual machines.

Let's take a deeper look into the components listed in the diagram above.
- **Physical Function (PF)** The PF is exposed as a virtual network adapter in the management operating system of the parent partition.
- **PF Miniport Driver** It is the PF miniport driver's responsibility to manage resources on the network adapter that are used by one or more VFs. The PF miniport driver is loaded in the management OS before any resources are allocated for a VF. If the PF miniport driver is halted, all the resources that were allocated for VFs will be freed.

- **Virtual Function (VF)** As we stated earlier, the VF is a lightweight PCIe function on a network adapter, and it supports the SR-IOV interface. The VF is associated with the VF on the network adapter and represents a virtualized intake of the network adapter. Each VF shares one or more physical resources on the NIC, for example the external network port.

- **VF Miniport Driver** The VF miniport driver is installed in the guest OS and is used to manage the VF.

- **Network Interface Card (NIC) Switch** The NIC switch is the hardware component of the network adapter that supports the SR-IOV interface. This forwards network traffic between the physical port and the internal virtual ports. Keep in mind that each Vport is attached to either a PF or VF.

- **Virtual Ports (VPorts)** A Vport is nothing more than a data object that is tied to an internal port on the NIC switch and supports the SR-IOV interface. This allows the transmission of packets to and from VFs or PFs.

- **Physical Port** This is the actual hardware's physical port that is used to connect the hardware to the external networking medium.

NOTE It is important to understand that VFs are hardware resources and because of this there are limitations on the number of VFs that are available on different hardware devices. Currently, such devices are offering up to 64 VFs per PF.

SR-IOV sounds great, but there are some caveats to using it. SR-IOV must be supported from the BIOS as well as the NIC and the operating system that is running Hypervisor. One thing that some people get a tad bit confused over is that Hyper-V does not require Second Level Address Translation (SLAT); however, for SR-IOV to work, SLAT is a requirement.

NOTE A device that is SR-IOV–capable can be used as a regular I/O device outside of virtualization.

Enabling SR-IOV

So this all sounds very interesting, but how do you enable it? Assuming that you have setup the BIOS correctly, your processors support SLAT, and you have an SR-IOV PCIe network card in the system, the first step to have any network connectivity (whether it is to enable SR-IOV or not) is to create an external virtual switch. You could do this by using the Virtual Switch Manager in Hyper-V Manager, or you could do this in PowerShell.

Let's start by looking at the Hyper-V Manager. You open Hyper-V Manager, then click Virtual Switch Manager on the right side of the screen. This opens the Virtual Switch Manager interface. From there it is much like creating any other virtual switch with one difference that you select the check box to enable SR-IOV:

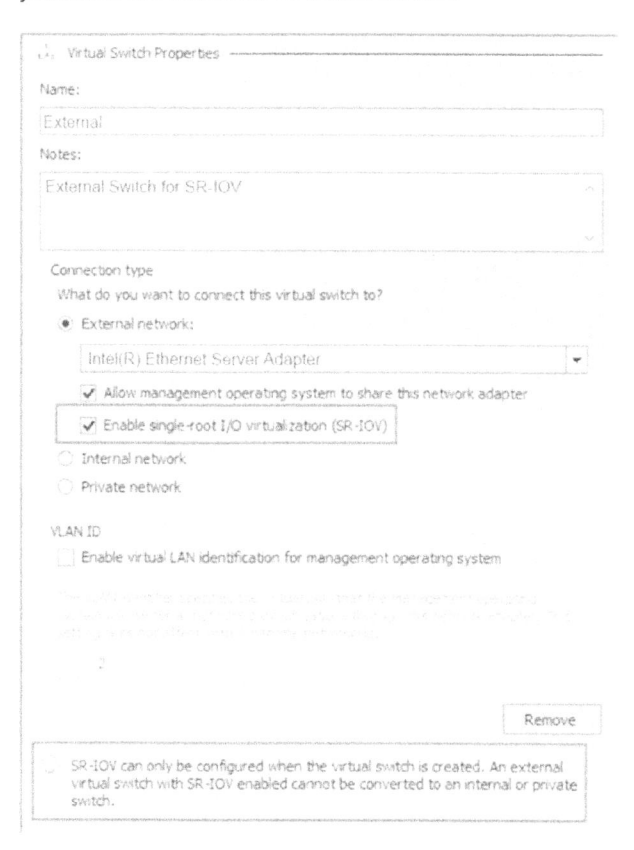

[Screenshot of Virtual Switch Properties dialog showing Name: External, Notes: External Switch for SR-IOV, Connection type set to External network with Intel(R) Ethernet Server Adapter selected, "Allow management operating system to share this network adapter" checked, "Enable single-root I/O virtualization (SR-IOV)" checked, and a note stating "SR-IOV can only be configured when the virtual switch is created. An external virtual switch with SR-IOV enabled cannot be converted to an internal or private switch."]

NOTE At the bottom of the Virtual Switch Properties window you can see the SR-IOV warning. Once a switch is created you cannot add this option again. If you want to add SR-IOV later you will have to delete the switch and recreate it.

As I suggested earlier, you can also create the virtual switch in PowerShell. Using PowerShell extensions for Hyper-V, you run the command New-VMSwitch. This command does require a parameter to specify the physical network that you want to use. For a list, run Get-NetAdapter.

The following screen shows a list of the network adapters in PowerShell:

```
PS C:\Users\administrator.KMNPIV> Get-NetAdapter
Name        InterfaceDescription                          ifIndex Status    MacAddress          LinkSpeed
----        --------------------                          ------- ------    ----------          ---------
Private     Broadcom NetXtreme Gigabit Ethernet #2         14     Up        00-1C-23-E1-71-FA    1 Gbps
HyperV      Broadcom BCM5709C NetXtreme II Gi...#29        15     Up        00-10-18-5B-05-1E    1 Gbps
Public      Broadcom NetXtreme Gigabit Ethernet            13     Up        00-1C-23-E1-71-FB    1 Gbps
SR-IOV      Broadcom BCM57712 NetXtreme...#26              12     Up        00-10-18-5B-05-1C    1 Gbps
```

After you have the network adapter's name, you can use the New-VMSwitch command:

```
PS C:\Users\administrator.KHNPIV> New-VMSwitch SR-IOV -netadaptername SR-IOV -EnableIov $true

Name             SwitchType  NetAdapterInterfaceDescription
----             ----------  ------------------------------
Sr-IOV           External    Broadcom BCM57712 NetXtreme...#26
```

The Get-VMSwitch command reveals the properties that were exposed on the VMNetworkadapter object:

```
PS C:\> get-vmswitch | fl "iov"

IovEnabled                : True
IovVirtualFunctionCount   : 32
IovVirtualFunctionsInUse  : 1
IovQueuePairCount         : 63
IovQueuePairsInUse        : 1
IovSupport                : True
IovSupportReasons         : {OK}
```

I know…that's cool, but what does it mean? Well, this is a great time to look at the output in greater detail.

At the top of the output is IovEnabled. This is true only when the virtual switch is created in SR-IOV mode…and false in any other configuration. The rest requires a bit more explanation:

- **IovVirtualFunctionCount** This is the number of VFs that are currently available for use by guest operating systems. Keep in mind this is a hardware setting on the physical network adapter and may vary by vendor. Also note that each software-based NIC can be backed by a VF. Also keep in mind that each VM can have up to eight software-based NICs.

- **IovVirtualFunctionsInUse** This is the current number of VFs in use by guest operating systems. In the screenshot above, this is listed as 1. This is because I have one VM that is running one NIC in SR-IOV mode.

- **IovQueuePairCount** This is the number of pairs that are available as hardware resources on the physical NIC. Again, this may vary from hardware vendor to hardware vendor. In most cases, there will be as many pairs available as there are VFs. Depending on the vendor, additional functionality might be included in the VFs, for instance a hardware vendor may support RSS in a guest operating system that is backed by a VF, and more than one queued pair may be required for this. Again this is all based on hardware, so any questions about this should be directed to the vendor.

- **IovQueuePairsInUse** This is the number of queued pairs that are currently assigned to VFs and assigned to a guest operating system.

The last two are similar. IovSupport and IovSupportReasons are numeric code and descriptions regarding the status of the physical network adapter. I will address this more in the "Troubleshooting SR-IOV" section.

Enabling the guest operating system

Now that the switch is created, is that it? The correct answer is not yet. You next have to enable the guest operating system. To do so, open the settings for the guest, expand the Network Adapter node, and click Hardware Acceleration. This is where you can enable SR-IOV for the guest:

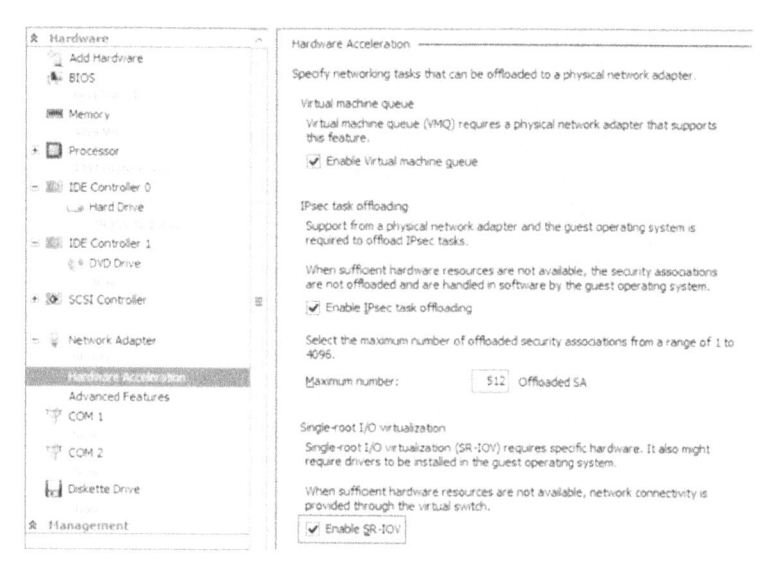

NOTE Selecting the Enable SR-IOV checkbox sets the IovWeight setting to some number greater than 0.

Now let's see how we can set this in PowerShell using the command Set-VMNetworkAdapter:

The screenshot above shows IovWeight set to 50. This requires some explanation. You might be familiar with VMQWeight in Windows Server 2008 R2. The IovWeight functionality operates the same in Windows Server 2012. This setting expresses the desire for a hardware offload, but it's not a guarantee. Any number greater than 0 turns this setting on. So, in short, 1 to 100 is on, and 0 is off.

> **NOTE** All numbers between 1 and 100 mean the same. This was put into the product specifically to allow for future expansion of a weighting system without the need to rewrite APIs.

Let's discuss some of the object attributes in the PowerShell output above:

- **IovQueuePairsRequested/IovQueuePairsAssigned** These two are for advanced networking features for a VF. My favorite advanced example is our good 'ole friend RSS. A software-based network adapter backed by a VF requires that the physical network adapter also supports RSS on a VF. So, by default IovQueuePairsRequested is set to 1; this should go without saying, but it can never be less than 1. If you have a VF that supports RSS and you have a multi-processor guest operating system, this setting would allow you to request additional queue pairs from the hardware to allow the guest operating system to scale. I should point out that this is only a request, and the actual number of queue pairs assigned may be less, again depending on the hardware. IovQueuePairsAssigned will always show the actual number of pair queues assigned.
- **IovInterruptModeration** With SR-IOV network cards, there are multiple functions (PFs and VFs) that process interrupts. IovInterruptModeration allows the VF driver to adapt depending on load. This functionality is implemented at the driver level and thus is up to the driver's vendor. So you should refer to the NIC vendor for any suggestions on this setting. Possible values are Default, Adaptive, Off, Low, Medium, and High.
- **IovUsage** If a VF is actively being used by a guest operating system, this value will be set to 1; otherwise it will be set to 0.
- **Status/StatusDescription** This is an array of numeric codes and descriptions that show the status of the network adapter. These codes and descriptions are not exclusive to SR-IOV, but we do populate them when IovWeight is set but not working correctly. More on this in the troubleshooting section.
- **VirtualFunction** This reveals a lot of information about the VF itself, but in almost all cases this can be safely ignored. It does provide a lot of data that might be useful to scripters, but that falls outside of this chapter's coverage.

Implementing network redundancy

We have covered a lot of SR-IOV information so far, and we are nearing the end. But there are a few more topics that I would like to go over. Windows Server 2012 introduces NIC teaming (also known as Load Balancing/Failover, or LBFO) natively. The very first thing to keep in mind about LBFO and SR-IOV is that when a team is created with SR-IOV–enabled NICs, the SR-IOV capability is not propagated upwards, so the two features are not compatible in the parent partition.

However, there is a solution for guest operating systems. If you require network redundancy with SR-IOV you can team the software NICs backed by VFs in the guest operating systems. There are some configuration suggestions to keep in mind for this. Each physical NIC, at the parent level, should be bound to a virtual switch (switch A and switch B) with SR-IOV enabled. The guest operating system should have two software network adapters. Network card A is connected to switch A, and network card B is connected to switch B. At the parent partition the network adapters *must* be configured to allow teaming. This can be accomplished by running the following command:

Get-VMNetworkAdapter –VMName "VMName" | Set-VMNetworkAdapter –AllowTeaming On

Configure the IovWeight, as described earlier, in the guest operating system. Finally, configure the teaming in the guest operating system in switch independent, address hash distribution mode.

You may be asking, What if I don't have two SR-IOV network cards? Can I still use teaming? The answer is yes, and it is supported. Keep in mind that LBFO does not understand that one NIC is backed by a VF and the other is not. So it could negate a non-optimal path to take that is not the VF backed NIC. To solve this you should configure the team for active/standby to ensure that the network card backed by a VF is active.

NOTE In Windows Server 2012 you can create a network team with up to 32 network cards, the support limit for a guest operating system is two, and this is not software enforced.

Troubleshooting SR-IOV

The time has come to discuss troubleshooting SR-IOV. We talked about the requirements to enable SR-IOV earlier in the chapter. Let's talk about a hypothetical situation where you have enabled SR-IOV on a switch in Hyper-V Virtual Switch Manager and enabled SR-IOV on a software network adapter in a guest operating system.

The most obvious place you will notice that SR-IOV is not working is in the Hyper-V Manager after selecting the Networking tab for a running virtual machine. Let's take a look.

IOV Broken Example

Adapter:	Network Adapter (Dynamic MAC: 00:15:5D:9F:FC:01)
Connection:	IOV
IP Addresses:	169.254.254.226, fe80::6cf9:9900:3d62:fee2
Status:	Degraded (SR-IOV not operational)

Summary | Memory | Networking | Replication

If you see the status shown in the above screenshot, you can be pretty sure that SR-IOV is not working. After seeing this indication, you should run the following PowerShell command to check the status of SR-IOV:

(Get-VMHost).IovSupportReasons

```
PS C:\> (Get-VMHost).IovSupportReasons
Ensure that the system has chipset support for SR-IOV and that I/O virtualization is enabled in the BIOS.
The chipset on the system does not do DMA remapping, without which SR-IOV cannot be supported.
The chipset on the system does not do interrupt remapping, without which SR-IOV cannot be supported.
SR-IOV cannot be used on this computer because the processor does not support second level address translation (SLAT).
For Intel processors, this feature might be referred to as Extended Page Tables (EPT). For AMD processors, this feature
might be referred to as Rapid Virtualization Indexing (RVI) or Nested Page Tables (NPT).
To use SR-IOV on this system, the system BIOS must be updated to allow Windows to control PCI Express. Contact your sys
tem manufacturer for an update.
SR-IOV cannot be used on this system as the PCI Express hardware does not support Access Control Services (ACS) at any
root port. Contact your system vendor for further information.
PS C:\> _
```

The resulting output is a pretty good description of why SR-IOV is not working.

In the following example you can see an output of a system where a chipset supports SR-IOV, but the BIOS does not. This is the most common error that you will see with SR-IOV:

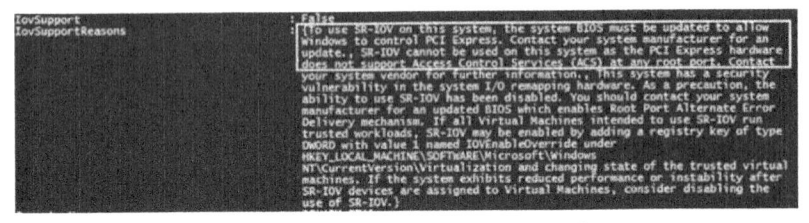

```
IovSupport        : False
IovSupportReasons : {To use SR-IOV on this system, the system BIOS must be updated to allow
                    Windows to control PCI Express. Contact your system manufacturer for an
                    update., SR-IOV cannot be used on this system as the PCI Express hardware
                    does not support Access Control Services (ACS) at any root port. Contact
                    your system vendor for further information. This system has a security
                    vulnerability in the system I/O remapping hardware. As a precaution, the
                    ability to use SR-IOV has been disabled. You should contact your system
                    manufacturer for an updated BIOS which enables Root Port Alternate Error
                    Delivery mechanism. If all Virtual Machines intended to use SR-IOV run
                    trusted workloads, SR-IOV may be enabled by adding a registry key of type
                    DWORD with value 1 named IOVEnableOverride under
                    HKEY_LOCAL_MACHINE\SOFTWARE\Microsoft\Windows
                    NT\CurrentVersion\Virtualization and changing state of the trusted virtual
                    machines. If the system exhibits reduced performance or instability after
                    SR-IOV devices are assigned to Virtual Machines, consider disabling the
                    use of SR-IOV.}
```

The error is highlighted in the screenshot above. As the output states, you must have a BIOS that allows Windows to control the PCI Express. To resolve this issue, you must contact your vendor to get an update to the BIOS that will enable the use of SR-IOV.

In this next snippet let's make some assumptions. First, let's assume you are running a system that has chipset support; second, you are using a BIOS that has support for SR-IOV; and third, you are using a network adapter that has SR-IOV capabilities. However, SR-IOV still is not working. The output of (Get-VMHost).IovSupportReasons could show the following:

```
IovSupport        : False
IovSupportReasons : {This system has a security vulnerability in the system I/O remapping
                    hardware. As a precaution, the ability to use SR-IOV has been disabled.
                    You should contact your system manufacturer for an updated BIOS which
                    enables Root Port Alternate Error Delivery mechanism. If all Virtual
                    Machines intended to use SR-IOV run trusted workloads, SR-IOV may be
                    enabled by adding a registry key of type DWORD with value 1 named
                    IOVEnableOverride under HKEY_LOCAL_MACHINE\SOFTWARE\Microsoft\Windows
                    NT\CurrentVersion\Virtualization and changing state of the trusted virtual
                    machines. If the system exhibits reduced performance or instability after
                    SR-IOV devices are assigned to Virtual Machines, consider disabling the
                    use of SR-IOV.}
```

Additionally, you may also notice an event in the Hyper-V SynthNic admin event log stating error 12607 occurred:

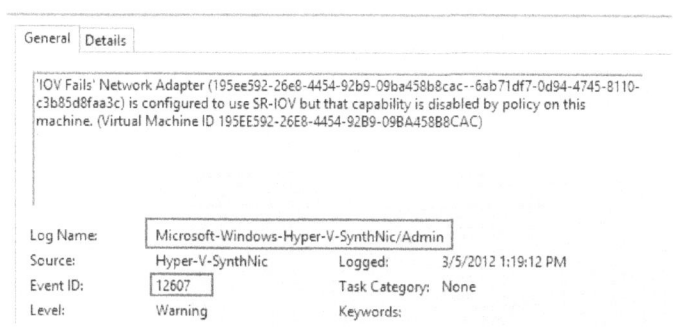

```
'IOV Fails' Network Adapter (195ee592-26e8-4454-92b9-09ba458b8cac--6ab71df7-0d94-4745-8110-
c3b85d8faa3c) is configured to use SR-IOV but that capability is disabled by policy on this
machine. (Virtual Machine ID 195EE592-26E8-4454-92B9-09BA458B8CAC)

Log Name:     Microsoft-Windows-Hyper-V-SynthNic/Admin
Source:       Hyper-V-SynthNic          Logged:         3/5/2012 1:19:12 PM
Event ID:     12607                     Task Category:  None
Level:        Warning                   Keywords:
```

Some explanation is in order. Even if you updated the BIOS for the SR-IOV base functionality, some chipsets have flaws in them. Some manufacturers are able to work around them, while some are not. These chipset flaws could cause the physical system to operate with reduced performance, or in the worst case, they could cause it to crash.

Get-NetAdapterSriov is another very useful cmdlet. This command gives you lots of useful information about the physical network adapter if it supports SR-IOV.

On a box that doesn't have support for SR-IOV, nothing gets returned as shown in the following screenshot:

```
PS C:\Windows\system32> Get-NetAdapterSriov
PS C:\Windows\system32>
```

The following screenshot shows output from a system that has an SR-IOV–capable network adapter:

```
PS C:\> Get-NetAdapterSriov Example | fl *

Caption                              :
Description                          :
ElementName                          : Example
InstanceID                           : Emulex OneConnect OCe11102-F, NIC/TOE
InterfaceDescription                 : Emulex OneConnect OCe11102-F, NIC/TOE
Name                                 : Example
Source                               : 2
SystemName                           :
CurrentCapabilities                  : MSFT_NetAdapterSriovCapabilities
Enabled                              : True
HardwareCapabilities                 : MSFT_NetAdapterSriovCapabilities
NumActiveDefaultVPortMacAddresses    : 1
NumActiveDefaultVPortVlanIds         : 0
NumActiveNonDefaultVPortMacAddresses : 1
NumActiveNonDefaultVPortVlanIds      : 0
NumActiveVPorts                      : 2
NumAllocatedVFs                      : 0
NumQueuePairsForDefaultVPort         : 1
NumQueuePairsForNonDefaultVPorts     : 16
NumVFs                               : 16
NumVPorts                            : 17
SriovSupport                         : 1
SwitchName                           : Default Switch
SwitchType                           : 1
PSComputerName                       :
ComputerName                         : JHOWARD-HEDT
ClassName                            : MSFT_NetAdapterSriovSettingData
Class                                : ROOT/StandardCimv2:MSFT_NetAdapterSriovSettingData
CimClass                             : ROOT/StandardCimv2:MSFT_NetAdapterSriovSettingData
Namespace                            : ROOT/StandardCimv2
Properties                           : {Caption, Description, ElementName, InstanceID...}
CimInstanceProperties                : {Caption, Description, ElementName, InstanceID...}
CimSystemProperties                  : Microsoft.Management.Infrastructure.CimSystemProperties
```

As look through all the objects that are returned, you can see that the NumVFs is 1, and this indicates that the network adapter is working and has available resources.

The next cmdlet that will assist you in troubleshooting issues is Get-VMswitch. Keep in mind that IovSupportReasons will display why SR-IOV is not functioning.

In the next example, you will see a system and a network adapter that do not support SR-IOV:

```
PS C:\Users\vmuser> Get-VMSwitch IOV | fl *

ComputerName                         : JHOWARD-GS
Name                                 : IOV
Id                                   : 073CDB37-7A18-4CF0-BE63-56785EBBB2A8
Notes                                :
SwitchType                           : External
AllowManagementOS                    : True
NetAdapterInterfaceDescription       : Broadcom BCM5708C NetXtreme II GigE (NDIS VBD Client) #44
AvailableVMQueues                    : 0
NumberVmqAllocated                   : 0
IovEnabled                           : True
IovVirtualFunctionCount              : 0
IovVirtualFunctionsInUse             : 0
IovQueuePairCount                    : 0
IovQueuePairsInUse                   : 0
AvailableIPSecSA                     : 0
NumberIPSecSAAllocated               : 0
BandwidthPercentage                  : 0
BandwidthReservationMode             : None
DefaultFlowMinimumBandwidthAbsolute  : 0
DefaultFlowMinimumBandwidthWeight    : 0
Extensions                           : {Microsoft NDIS Capture, Microsoft Windows Filtering Platform}
IovSupport                           : False
IovSupportReasons                    : {Ensure that the system has chipset support for SR-IOV and that I/O
                                       virtualization is enabled in the BIOS., The chipset on the system does not do
                                       DMA remapping, without which SR-IOV cannot be supported., The chipset on the
                                       system does not do interrupt remapping, without which SR-IOV cannot be
                                       supported., SR-IOV cannot be used on this computer because the processor does
                                       not support second level address translation (SLAT). For Intel processors, this
                                       feature might be referred to as Extended Page Tables (EPT). For AMD processors,
                                       this feature might be referred to as Rapid Virtualization Indexing (RVI) or
                                       Nested Page Tables (NPT)....}
IsDeleted                            : False
```

The following is an example of a system that does support SR-IOV but has a network adapter that does not:

```
PS D:\> Get-VMSwitch "Not-In-IOV-Mode" | fl *

ComputerName                         : JHOWARD-G7
Name                                 : Not-In-IOV-Mode
Id                                   : 5A474A69-7140-4EF8-9D26-841450864E95
Notes                                :
SwitchType                           : External
AllowManagementOS                    : True
NetAdapterInterfaceDescription       : Broadcom BCM5709C NetXtreme II GigE (NDIS VBD Client) #60
AvailableVMQueues                    : 0
NumberVmqAllocated                   : 0
IovEnabled                           : False
IovVirtualFunctionCount              : 0
IovVirtualFunctionsInUse             : 0
IovQueuePairCount                    : 0
IovQueuePairsInUse                   : 0
AvailableIPSecSA                     : 0
NumberIPSecSAAllocated               : 0
BandwidthPercentage                  : 10
BandwidthReservationMode             : Absolute
DefaultFlowMinimumBandwidthAbsolute  : 12500000
DefaultFlowMinimumBandwidthWeight    : 0
Extensions                           : {Microsoft NDIS Capture, Microsoft Windows Filtering Platform}
IovSupport                           : False
IovSupportReasons                    : {This network adapter does not support SR-IOV.}
IsDeleted                            : False
```

Notice that the IovSupportReasons clearly points out that the network adapter does not support SR-IOV.

Below is another system that supports SR-IOV. The network adapter also supports SR-IOV; however, the switch was not created in SR-IOV mode:

```
PS D:\> Get-VMSwitch "Not-In-IOV-Mode" | fl *

ComputerName                       : JHOWARD-G7
Name                               : Not-In-IOV-Mode
Id                                 : C313E75D-4C17-4978-9805-497DAF4EEED4
Notes                              :
SwitchType                         : External
AllowManagementOS                  : True
NetAdapterInterfaceDescription     : Broadcom BCM57712 NetXtreme II 10 GigE Dual Port SFP+ Adapter (NDIS VBD Client)
AvailableVMQueues                  : #73
NumberVmqAllocated                 : 14
IovEnabled                         : 1
IovVirtualFunctionCount            : False
IovVirtualFunctionsInUse           : 0
IovQueuePairCount                  : 0
IovQueuePairsInUse                 : 0
AvailableIPSecSA                   : 0
NumberIPSecSAAllocated             : 0
BandwidthPercentage                : 10
BandwidthReservationMode           : Absolute
DefaultFlowMinimumBandwidthAbsolute: 125000000
DefaultFlowMinimumBandwidthWeight  : 0
Extensions                         : {Microsoft NDIS Capture, Microsoft Windows Filtering Platform}
IovSupport                         : True
IovSupportReasons                  : {OK}
IsDeleted                          : False
```

This situation might be a bit tricky to notice. IovSupport and IovSupportReasons look good, but closer examination shows that IovVirtualFunctionCount is 0. Now compare that to the output from a good system and notice the difference:

```
PS C:\> get-vmswitch IOV | fl *

ComputerName                       : JHOWARD-HEDT
Name                               : IOV
Id                                 : 707D1E93-4E6E-44E5-8449-29AA57CAC946
Notes                              :
SwitchType                         : External
AllowManagementOS                  : True
NetAdapterInterfaceDescription     : Intel(R) Ethernet Server Adapter X520-2 #2
AvailableVMQueues                  : 31
NumberVmqAllocated                 : 0
IovEnabled                         : True
IovVirtualFunctionCount            : 32
IovVirtualFunctionsInUse           : 0
IovQueuePairCount                  : 63
IovQueuePairsInUse                 : 1
AvailableIPSecSA                   : 2048
NumberIPSecSAAllocated             : 0
BandwidthPercentage                : 0
BandwidthReservationMode           : None
DefaultFlowMinimumBandwidthAbsolute: 0
DefaultFlowMinimumBandwidthWeight  : 0
Extensions                         : {Microsoft NDIS Capture, Microsoft Windows Filtering Platform}
IovSupport                         : True
IovSupportReasons                  : {OK}
IsDeleted                          : False
```

Earlier in this section, I mentioned the IovVirtualFunctionCount object. In case you have forgotten, this is the number of VFs that are currently available for use by guest operating systems. If this number is 0, the most likely cause is that the switch was not created with SR-IOV support.

If you enable any of the network policies, like RouterGuard, the parent OS will force the virtual machine to go through the VMbus and not use SR-IOV so that the policies are applied. If all else looks like it should work, but SR-IOV is still not working, check the virtual machine for network policies and remove them.

Also remember that SR-IOV is only a Windows Server-based feature. So if you are running Hyper-V in the Windows 8 client, you will not be able to enable SR-IOV.

—*Keith Hill, Senior Support Escalation Engineer, Windows Server Core High Availability Team*

Additional resources

Here are a few additional resources concerning this topic:

- Overview of Single Root I/O Virtualization (SR-IOV) (Windows Dev Center - Hardware) at:
  http://msdn.microsoft.com/en-us/library/windows/hardware/hh440148(v=vs.85).aspx
- Hyper-V Support for Scaling Up and Scaling Out Overview (TechNet Library) at:
  http://technet.microsoft.com/en-us/library/hh831389.aspx

N_Port ID Virtualization

N_Port ID Virtualization (NPIV) is a technology available in a Fibre Channel (FC) storage area network (SAN) that allows multiple N_Port IDs to share a single physical N_Port on the SAN. NPIV uses Host Bus Adapter (HBA) technology to create virtual HBA ports on hosts by abstracting the underlying physical port. This allows a single physical Fibre Channel HBA port to function as multiple logical ports, each having its own identity. Different virtual machines can then attach themselves to their own virtual HBA ports so they can be independently zoned to a distinct and dedicated World Wide Port Name (WWPN) on the SAN.

The Virtual Fibre Channel feature of Windows Server 2012 Hyper-V uses the existing NPIV T11 standard to map multiple virtual N_Port IDs to a single physical Fibre Channel N_port for a Hyper-V guest. A new NPIV port is created on the host each time you start a virtual machine that is configured with a virtual HBA. When the virtual machine stops running on the host, the NPIV port is removed.

In this section, Keith Hill, a Senior Support Escalation Engineer with the Windows Server Core High Availability Team, provides some step-by-step guidance on setting up NPIV with Virtual Fibre Channel to help you ensure that your configuration is optimized and won't have problems. Keith also had help from Tina Chapman from the Lab group for this section, who assisted in setting up a lab for NPIV and aided in developing the documentation.

Synthetic FC and NPIV

Before Windows Server 2012, Hyper-V allowed storage connectivity to IDE (VHD and VHDX files) and SCSI disk (VHD and VHDX files), and attaching to iSCSI disk on an iSCSI target server. Microsoft has since understood customers' needs for more storage options. Many of our customers have spent a great deal on storage solutions that utilize fibre connections such as SAN storage. Windows Server 2012 introduces a new storage connection solution that allows users to connect virtual machines directly to the extensive storage infrastructure. Utilizing N_Port ID Virtualization (NPIV), Windows Server now offers Synthetic Fibre Channel storage connection.

Some of the key features of virtual Fiber Channel (synthetic FC) are:

- Allows the use of NPIV
- Provides unmitigated access to your SAN
- Provides hardware-based I/O path to the Windows software virtual hard disk stack

- Allows you to have a single Hyper-V host connected to different SANs with multiple Fibre Channel ports
- Can have up to four virtual HBAs in the guest OS
- Allows you to use MPIO to ensure high availability connections to your storage

Synthetic FC allows a guest operating system to use a WWN that is associated with it to directly connect to the SAN. This allows for the virtualization of workloads that require SAN-connected LUNs. The Synthetic FC also allows new virtualization scenarios, such as guest clustering with FC SAN-attached storage. In previous operating systems, this was only accomplished by using iSCSI connectivity to shared storage.

In order to use a synthetic FC adapter in the guest operating system you must first understand what is required. The first step is that your SAN must support NPIV (an ANSI T11 Standard), switches must support NPIV, and your HBA cards must support NPIV. The host operating system must be running Windows Server 2012, and the guest must be running Windows Server 2008, Windows Server 2008 R2, or Windows Server 2012. NPIV allows a Fibre Channel HBA to function as multiple logical ports. It does this by creating a new virtual WWNN and WWPN pair on the physical HBA.

NPIV supports migration of these new WWNNs and WWPNs from one HBA to another HBA that could be located on another physical host. NPIV does this by migrating the synthetic FC ports from an HBA on the source host to an HBA on the target host when a guest operating system is migrated. I shouldn't have to say that this would be an administrative nightmare if this would have to be done by hand, without NPIV.

The main components of synthetic FC are:

- **Fibre Channel Virtual Device (VDEV)** This runs at the host level.
- **Virtual Services Provider (VSP)** This runs at the host level.
- **Virtual Services Client (VSC)** This runs at the guest level.

In a diagram at a high level, it would look something like this:

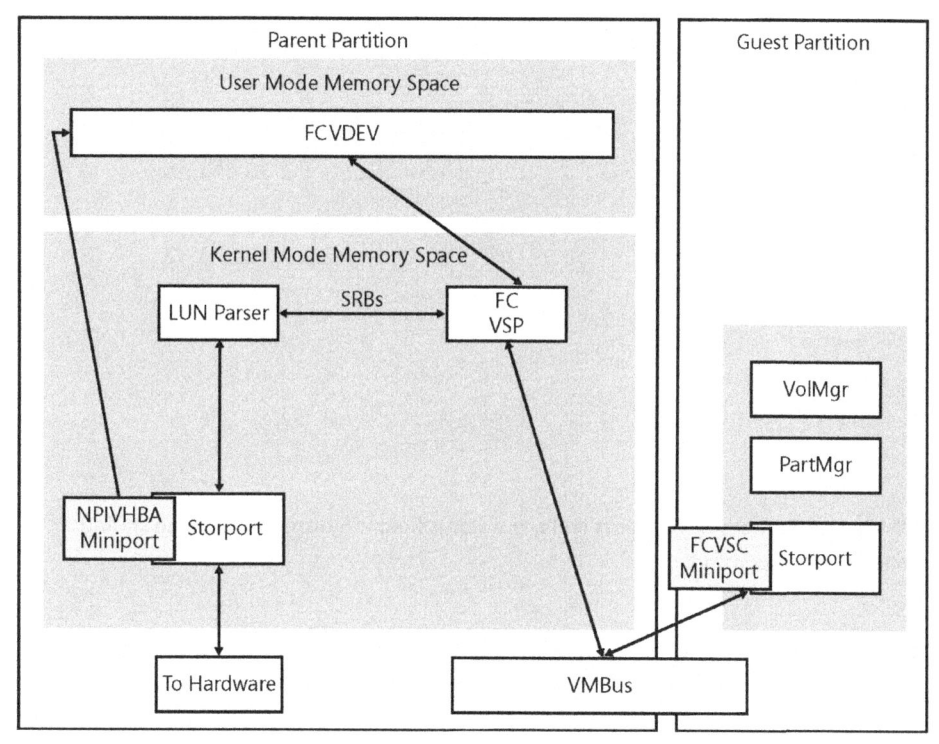

On the Parent Partition (host) a virtual port (vPort) is created. The LUN is associated with that vPort, which is the WWNN and the WWPN. Think of it like a MAC address for Ethernet. The LUNs are loaded onto the Parent Partition's storage stack, and the synthetic FC then surfaces a physical device object (PDO) inside the guest operating system and links it to the SCSI PDO that was created on the Parent Partition.

NOTE Each Guest can have up to four virtual Fibre Channel Adapters.

That's all good to know, but is there anything more, you ask? Well, let's look at how to setup a synthetic FC.

Assuming that you have NPIV enabled and capable devices (SAN, Switches, HBAs), first open Hyper-V Manager and click Virtual SAN Manager in the Actions pane:

Actions

LC2-12H07
- New
- Import Virtual Machine...
- Hyper-V Settings...
- Virtual Switch Manager...
- Virtual SAN Manager...
- Edit Disk...
- Inspect Disk...
- Stop Service
- Remove Server
- Refresh
- View
- Help

NOTE If your HBA does not support NPIV, the status field will display a message stating that NPIV is not supported.

NOTE If you are configuring this on a failover cluster, ensure that both the new Virtual Fibre Channel SAN name and the Global Fibre Channel Settings are identical for each node.

After the Virtual SAN Manager window opens, you should see the following:

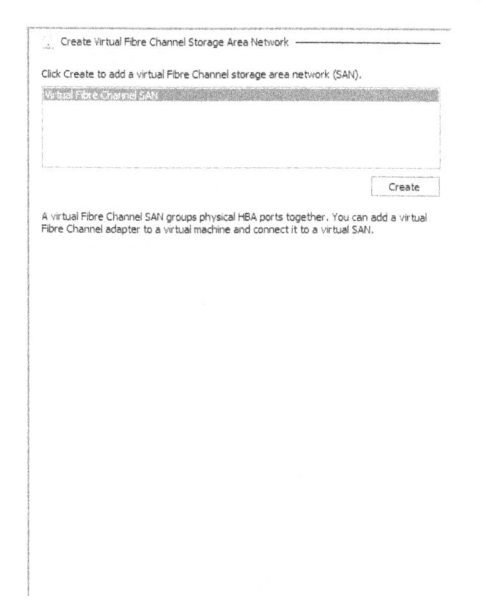

In the next window, select the WWNN, define a name for the new virtual SAN, and add some notes for easier identification later:

The WWNN listed for the HBA. Select the one that you want to use for the virtual SAN. Since there is only one WWNN for this example, I will select it:

Click OK to view the World Wide Names under the Global Fibre Channel Settings:

The address range here is default. You can, however, change the maximum and minimum settings as needed.

When you have that set up, begin adding Fibre Channel Adapters to your guest operating systems. To do this, first turn off the guest operating system and go to the settings for the guest. Click Add Hardware, select Fibre Channel Adapter, and click Add:

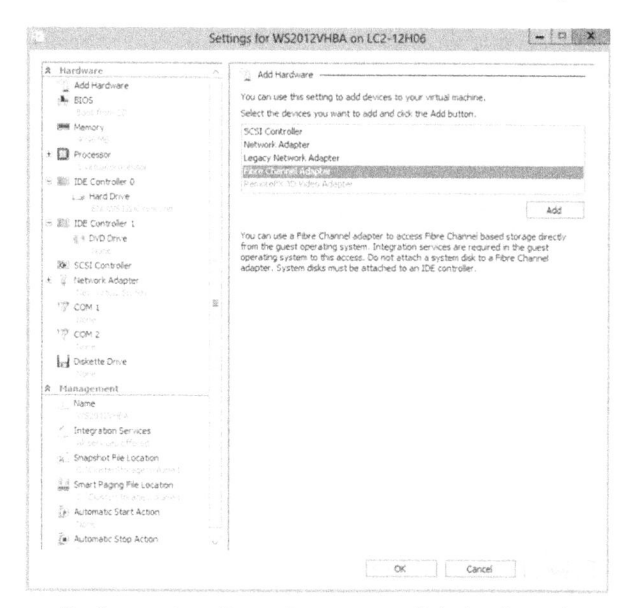

On the next configuration screen, click the drop-down arrow under Virtual SAN, click the name of the virtual Fibre Channel SAN you created, and then click Apply.

> **NOTE** Make a note of the WWPNs for both Address Set A and Address set B. You will use these WWPNs to zone your LUNs to this guest operating system.

> **NOTE** If you have more than one guest operating system in a failover cluster using synthetic FCs, each of them will need unique WWNNs.

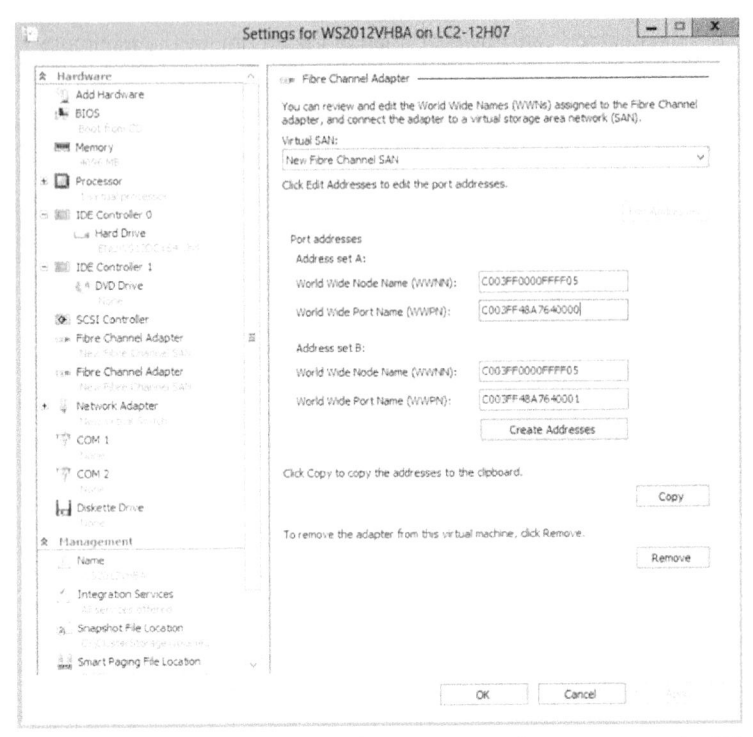

[Screenshot: Settings for WS2012VHBA on LC2-12H07 — Fibre Channel Adapter configuration]

At this point, you can turn on the guest operating systems again. When the guest operating system comes up, verify that the Fibre Channel HBAs are visible in Device Manager:

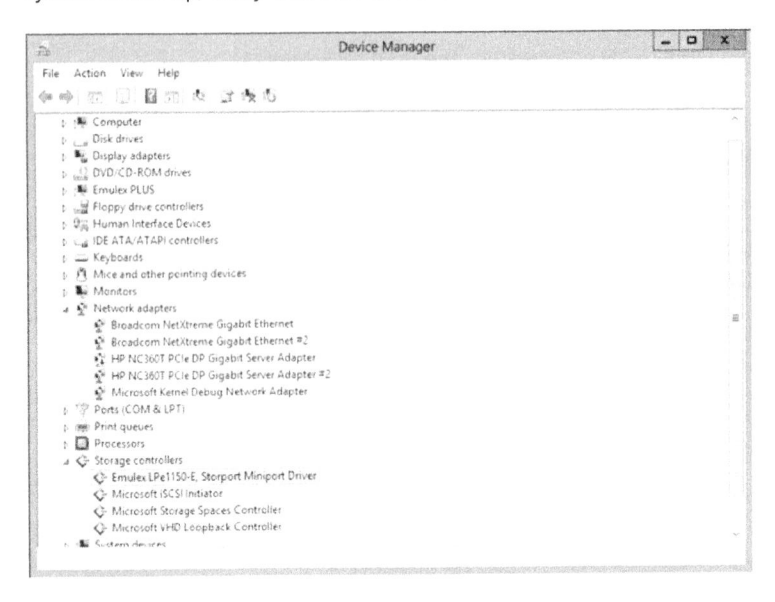

[Screenshot: Device Manager showing storage controllers including Emulex LPe1150-E, Storport Miniport Driver]

NOTE If you are running Windows Server 2008 R2 and the synthetic FCs are not showing up, ensure that you have installed the latest integrated services to the guest operating system.

Two of the WWPNs should now be visible in your SAN fabric.

NOTE Depending on your fabric topology, complete any required steps to add all four WWPNs to a zone.

The following screenshot shows that I have four back end ports configured from Compellent SAN in an alias and the four WWPNs from the guest operating system in a separate alias with both of the aliases in a zone set:

NOTE The physical HBA from each cluster node is not included in the zone set.

If you are using MPIO you will need to configure that in the guest operating system and to see your storage from the SAN within the guest.

—Keith Hill, Sr. Support Escalation Engineer, Windows Server Core High Availability Team

—Tina Chapman, Lab Engineer, US-CSS CC Labs

Additional resources

Here are a few additional resources concerning this topic:
- Hyper-V Virtual Fibre Channel Overview (TechNet Library) at: http://technet.microsoft.com/en-us/library/hh831413.aspx
- Super-fast Failovers with VM Machine Guest Clustering in Windows Server 2012 Hyper-V (IT Pros ROCK! at Microsoft) at: http://blogs.technet.com/b/keithmayer/archive/2013/03/21/virtual-machine-guest-clustering-with-windows-server-2012-become-a-virtualization-expert-in-20-days-part-14-of-20.aspx

Failover cluster networking

Failover Clustering is a Windows Server feature that can provide high availability and scalability to different kinds of server workloads, including Microsoft Exchange Server, Hyper-V, Microsoft SQL Server, and file servers. These server applications can run on physical servers or on virtual machines running on Hyper-V hosts.

Failover Clustering has been enhanced in Windows Server 2012 with support for increased scalability, continuously available file-based server application storage, easier management, faster failover, and more flexible architectures for implementing failover clusters. Failover clustering is a big subject that could merit an entire book of its own, but here we'll focus only on the networking side of failover clusters.

Subhasish Bhattacharya, a Program Manager with the Clustering and High Availability team at Microsoft, outlines a number of considerations for configuring your cluster network to ensure resiliency and quality of service. He also examines how to optimize cluster health monitoring for transient cluster network failures and describes which networks are used for cluster shared volume (CSV) redirected traffic.

Considerations when configuring your cluster network

This section summarizes some configuration tips for ensuring resiliency and network quality of service (QoS) of failover cluster networking for Windows Server 2012 hosts.

Resiliency

In a highly available system the goal is to avoid any single point of failure. To ensure resiliency in the network of a failover cluster, make sure that you do the following:

- Use multiple physical NICs rather than carving up all VLANs to the same switch.
- Connect NICs to different switches.
- Use NIC Teaming for network resiliency. This is most important for non-redundant networks, such as for client connectivity. Intra-cluster communication, CSV, and Live Migration will failover to another network on failure.
- Use different types of NICs for your cluster network. This ensures that a driver bug in a particular type of NIC will not impact all connectivity.
- Ensure upstream network resiliency. Eliminate a single point of failure between multiple networks.

Network Quality of Service

Cluster heartbeats are lightweight but sensitive to latency. If a heartbeat cannot get through, it might be falsely interpreted that the nodes are down. To ensure network quality of service for failover clustering, make sure that you do the following:

- Use multiple network cards.
- Create VLANs.
- Turn on the new Windows Server 2012 QoS settings for Prioritization and Bandwidth Allocation as follows:
    - Prioritization: It is recommended that the QoS Priority Flow Control policy is set for all cluster deployments to ensure that intra-cluster communication is sent first. To configure using Windows PowerShell:

    New-NetQosPolicy "Cluster"-IPDstPort 3343 –Priority 6

    - Bandwidth Allocation: It is recommended that the Relative Minimum Bandwidth SMB policy is set for CSV deployments. Here is an example of setting this using Windows PowerShell:

    New-NetQosPolicy –Name "SMB policy" –SMB –MinBandwidthWeightAction 50

Optimizing cluster health monitoring for transient cluster network failures

Windows Server Failover Clustering by default is configured to deliver the highest levels of availability by quickly detecting and reacting to failures. If a node is not reachable over the network, recovery action is taken to recover and bring applications and services online on another node in the cluster. However, in some instances this can result in premature failovers during transient cluster network failures.

To accomplish a fast recovery from hard failures, such as the complete loss of a server, the default settings for cluster health monitoring are fairly aggressive. These settings are fully configurable and can be increased to decrease the sensitivity of the cluster monitoring to transient cluster network failures. The tradeoff is that unrecoverable, hard failures result in greater downtimes. It is also important to realize that relaxing the health monitoring settings does not fix network problems; it only masks them.

The following are some details concerning cluster health monitoring properties:

- **SameSubnetDelay** Frequency heartbeats are sent:
    - Default: 1 second
    - Relaxed: 1 second
    - Maximum: 2 seconds

- **SameSubnetThreshold** Missed heartbeats before an interface is considered down:
  - Default: 5 heartbeats
  - Relaxed: 10 heartbeats
  - Maximum: 120 heartbeats
- **CrossSubnetDelay** Frequency heartbeats are sent to nodes on dissimilar subnets:
  - Default: 1 second
  - Relaxed: 2 seconds
  - Maximum: 4 seconds
- **CrossSubnetThreshold** Missed heartbeats before an interface is considered down to nodes on dissimilar subnets:
  - Default: 5 heartbeats
  - Relaxed: 10 heartbeats
  - Maximum: 120 heartbeats

To view the current heartbeat configuration values using Windows PowerShell use the Get-Cluster cmdlet:

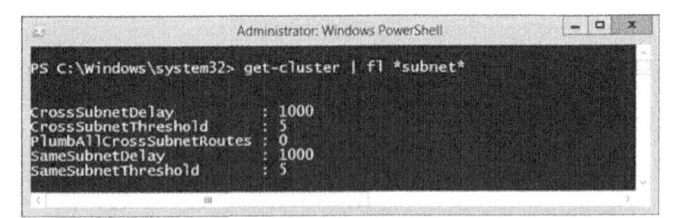

```
PS C:\Windows\system32> get-cluster | fl *subnet*

CrossSubnetDelay           : 1000
CrossSubnetThreshold       : 5
PlumbAllCrossSubnetRoutes  : 0
SameSubnetDelay            : 1000
SameSubnetThreshold        : 5
```

The heartbeat configuration values can be modified using the Get-Cluster cmdlet:

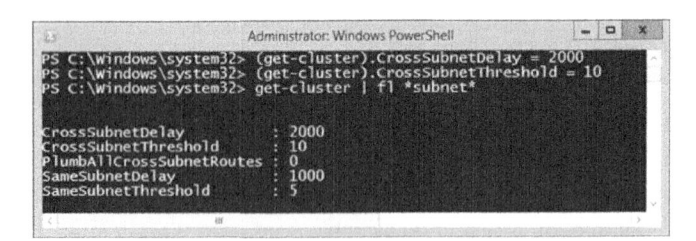

```
PS C:\Windows\system32> (get-cluster).CrossSubnetDelay = 2000
PS C:\Windows\system32> (get-cluster).CrossSubnetThreshold = 10
PS C:\Windows\system32> get-cluster | fl *subnet*

CrossSubnetDelay           : 2000
CrossSubnetThreshold       : 10
PlumbAllCrossSubnetRoutes  : 0
SameSubnetDelay            : 1000
SameSubnetThreshold        : 5
```

Which networks are used for CSV redirected traffic?

In Windows Server 2012, cluster shared volume (CSV) is integrated with SMB Multichannel. This enables CSV redirected traffic to be streamed across multiple networks in parallel, resulting in an improved I/O performance. CSV traffic will default to SMB Multichannel and failover to NetFT if SMB Multichannel is not available.

The next two sections explain the CSV network selection flow for the different file sharing protocols available.

SMB Multichannel

SMB Multichannel is the default file sharing protocol for CSV. The following table summarizes the NIC selection rules and logic for this scenario:

NIC SELECTION RULE	SELECTION LOGIC
NICs are enabled for cluster use.	NICs that are set for internal cluster communication are selected first. The UseClientAccessNetworksForSharedVolumes Cluster property can be additionally set to ensure that a NIC is considered for CSV traffic.
NICs have the best features.	RDMA-capable NICs are selected first. If none are available RSS-capable and/or teamed NIC are picked. If neither of these NICs are available others are selected.
NICs have the highest speed.	If multiple networks meet the three selection criteria for SMB Multichannel then CSV traffic is streamed in parallel over them.

NetFT

NetFT is used whenever SMB Multichannel is not available. The following table summarizes the NIC selection rules and logic for this scenario:

NIC SELECTION RULE	SELECTION LOGIC
Cluster Network Prioritization metric	The cluster networks selected by NetFT to stream traffic will be determined by their Network Prioritization metric. The network with the lowest metric will be selected for CSV traffic. The value of a cluster network metric can be set using the following Windows PowerShell cmdlet: PS> (Get-ClusterNetwork "<Network Name>").Metric = <Metric Value>

—*Subhasish Bhattacharya, Program Manager, Clustering and High Availability*

Additional resources

Here is an additional resource concerning this topic:

- Network Performance and Availability (TechNet Library) at: http://technet.microsoft.com/en-us/library/hh831499.aspx

SMB Multichannel and CSV

SMB Multichannel is one of several new features in version 3.0 of the Server Message Block (SMB) protocol introduced in Windows Server 2012. SMB Multichannel allows multiple connections to be used within a single SMB session in order to enhance network performance and ensure greater availability of file shares on Windows servers.

Cluster shared volumes (CSV) were introduced with Windows Server 2008 R2 and allow each node that is part of the same Windows Failover Cluster to access the same disk (LUN) at the same time. CSV allows virtual machines to fail over independent from each other. CSV has also been enhanced in various ways in Windows Server 2012.

In this section, Cristian Edwards Sabathe, EMEA PFE Regional Workload Lead for Server Virtualization, explains how SMB Multichannel and CSV can work together in Windows Server 2012. He also compares the cluster network roles and metrics between Windows Server 2012 and the earlier Windows Server 2008 R2 platform.

Windows Server 2012 SMB Multichannel and CSV Redirected traffic caveats

Cluster shared volumes (CSV) was introduced with Windows Server 2008 R2 to enable simultaneous access to the same LUN from several Hyper-V hosts, using a common name space under C:\ClusterStorage and allowing storage of several virtual machines by providing them with high availability and Live Migration without moving the LUN from one host to another.

In addition to simplifying and centralizing the management of virtual machines, CSV volumes increase fault tolerance, allowing redirect access to the LUN through cluster networks to the coordinator node, in the event that any of the nodes lose direct connectivity with the SAN. This, for example, allows continued service to the virtual machines hosted on a Hyper-V server that loses connectivity to storage, since you can redirect disk access through cluster networks until connectivity is restored with the SAN.

The main intention of this article is to cover and explain how the new Windows Server 2012 Failover Cluster manages the CSV Networks and the SMB Multichannel together.

The new way: Windows Server 2012 cluster network roles and metrics

In Windows Server 2012 Failover Clusters, the philosophy of the metrics and the roles of cluster networks is maintained. So, there are still external, internal, and excluded networks, but the value of the metrics by default change substantially for a better integration with the new SMB Multichannel functionality. In Windows Server 2008 R2, the CSV traffic could be redirected by a single physical network adapter, but in Windows Server 2012, the CSV traffic can be redirected using more than one network adapter simultaneously by taking advantage of SMB Multichannel.

However, if by any restrictions of your environment, you want to ensure that you use only the network with the lower metric, you must understand how the cluster in Windows Server 2012 determines that CSV traffic is redirected.

The following information describes how Windows Server 2012 assigns metrics automatically to the cluster networks on the basis not only of the role, but the functionality of the physical network card.

- **External Network (role 3)** Metrics are assigned automatically as follows:
  - **Metric** Starting at 80,000
  - **Default gateway** Yes
  - **If RDMA capable** -19,000
  - **If RSS capable** -9,600
  - **NetFT Link Speed (1 GB at least)** -(16 * network card link speed in gigabytes)
- **Internal Network (role 1)** Metrics are assigned automatically as follows:
  - **Metric** Starting at 40,000
  - **Default gateway** No
  - **If RDMA capable** -19,000
  - **If RSS capable** -9,600
  - **NetFT Link Speed (1 GB at least)** -(16 * network card link speed in gigabytes)
- **Excluded Cluster Network (role 0)** Metrics are assigned automatically as follows:
  - **Metric** Starting at 80,000
  - **Default gateway** No
  - **If RDMA capable** -19,000
  - **If RSS capable** -9,600
  - **NetFT Link Speed (1 GB at least)** -(16 * network card link speed in gigabytes)

NOTE For all three types of networks, RSS will not be subtracted from the metric if the adapter is RDMA capable. If the second and next external cards have the same value, the cluster will increase the final metric value by one for these additional external networks.

Let's consider a real example in Windows Server 2012 to better understand how this formula applies to your environment.

In the screenshot below is a cluster with five networks (Contoso_Mgmt, Contoso_Cluster, iSCSI, Live Migration, and Slow) and the metrics that have been automatically assigned once the cluster was created:

- Network Contoso_Mgmt is external and the cluster automatically assigns the 70,240 metric.

  This is because the physical adapter is not RDMA but is RSS capable with a 10-GB link speed (80,000 – 9,600 – 160 = 70,240).

- The Live Migration network is the first detected internal network from when the cluster was created and has the autometric of 30,240.

  This is because the physical adapter is not RDMA but is RSS capable with a 10-GB link speed (40,000 – 9,600 – 160 = 30,240).

- The second internal network, Contoso_Cluster, has the autometric of 30,240 + 1.

  This is because the physical adapter is not RDMA but is RSS capable with a 10-GB link speed (40,000 – 9,600 – 160 + 1 = 30,241).

- The third internal network, Slow, has the autometric of 40,000.

  This is because the physical adapter is not RDMA and RSS capable and the link speed is 100 MB. The NetFT subtract is not applied because the adapter must be at least 1 GB.

NOTE Windows Server 2012 does not support 100-MB physical NICs, and this example is only for the purpose of understanding the formula.

- The iSCSI network is automatically detected and excluded from the cluster networks. The metric assigned (70,241) will be the biggest and not used for cluster communications.

   This is because the physical adapter is not RDMA but is RSS capable with a 10-GB link speed (80,000 − 9,600 − 160 + 1 = 70,241).

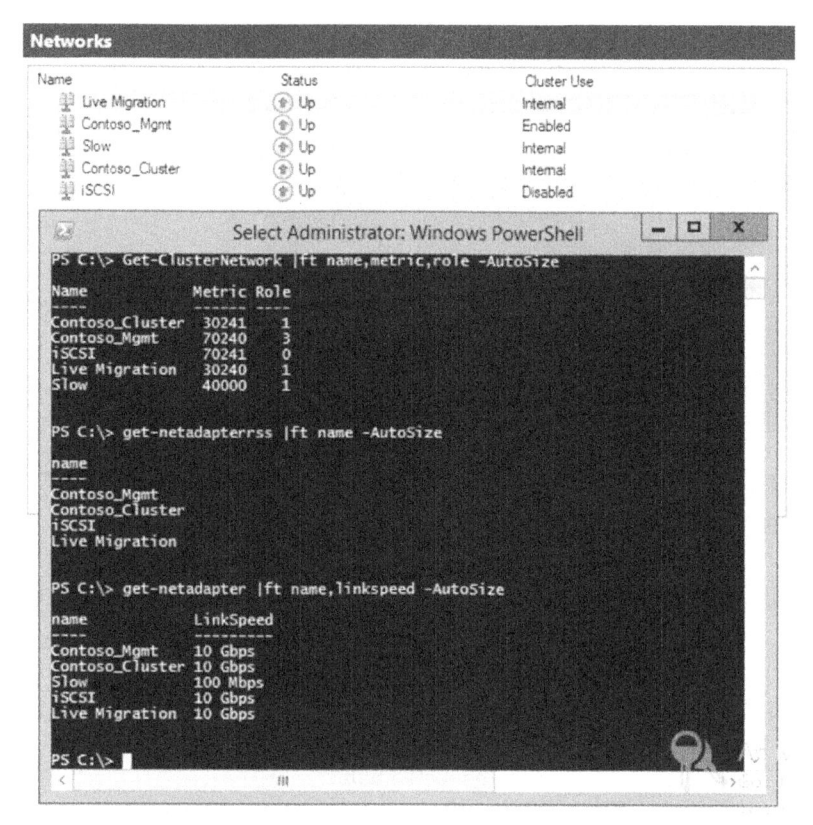

```
Networks

Name                     Status       Cluster Use
   Live Migration        Up           Internal
   Contoso_Mgmt          Up           Enabled
   Slow                  Up           Internal
   Contoso_Cluster       Up           Internal
   iSCSI                 Up           Disabled
```

```
Select Administrator: Windows PowerShell

PS C:\> Get-ClusterNetwork |ft name,metric,role -AutoSize

Name             Metric  Role
----             ------  ----
Contoso_Cluster  30241   1
Contoso_Mgmt     70240   3
iSCSI            70241   0
Live Migration   30240   1
Slow             40000   1


PS C:\> get-netadapterrss |ft name -AutoSize

name
----
Contoso_Mgmt
Contoso_Cluster
iSCSI
Live Migration


PS C:\> get-netadapter |ft name,linkspeed -AutoSize

name             LinkSpeed
----             ---------
Contoso_Mgmt     10 Gbps
Contoso_Cluster  10 Gbps
Slow             100 Mbps
iSCSI            10 Gbps
Live Migration   10 Gbps

PS C:\>
```

In the above configuration, the Live Migration cluster network has the lowest metric, and perhaps this is a configuration that you don't want for your environment.

If so you can manually change the metrics and assign the lowest metric to the Contoso_Cluster cluster network:

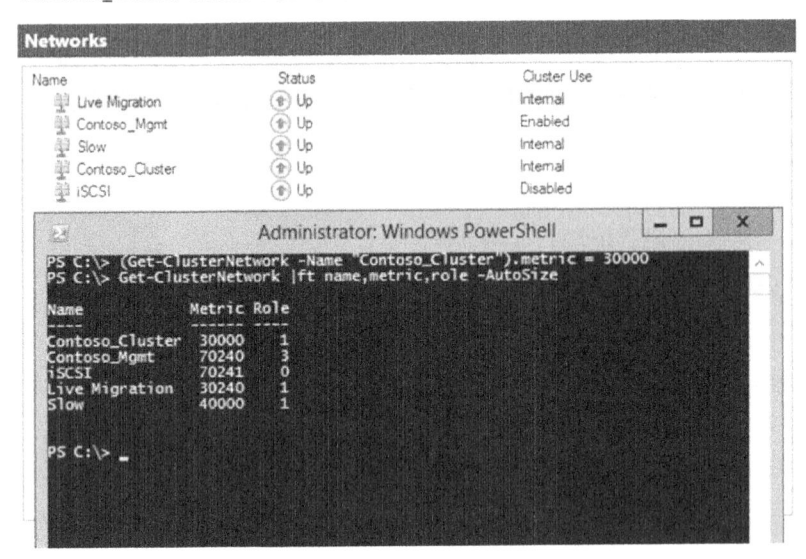

```
Networks
Name                    Status      Cluster Use
 Live Migration          Up          Internal
 Contoso_Mgmt            Up          Enabled
 Slow                    Up          Internal
 Contoso_Cluster         Up          Internal
 iSCSI                   Up          Disabled
```

```
Administrator: Windows PowerShell
PS C:\> (Get-ClusterNetwork -Name "Contoso_Cluster").metric = 30000
PS C:\> Get-ClusterNetwork |ft name,metric,role -AutoSize

Name              Metric Role
----              ------ ----
Contoso_Cluster    30000    1
Contoso_Mgmt       70240    3
iSCSI              70241    0
Live Migration     30240    1
Slow               40000    1

PS C:\>
```

How SMB Multichannel changes the behavior to select the CSV cluster network

In the example above, the Contoso_Cluster cluster network now has the lowest metric, but does this means that this will be the only adapter used for CSV redirected traffic? The answer is no! The metrics don't apply in Windows Server 2012 by default because SMB Multichannel is enabled by default as well. So let's figure out what subnets or cluster networks will be used in this particular case applying these rules:

- **Rule 1** SMB Multichannel takes precedence over the Network Priorities of NetFT to decide what subnets to use for the CSV redirected traffic.

- **Rule 2** The cluster will use only internal cluster networks by default for SMB Multichannel. This behavior can be changed to also use the external networks modifying the UseClientAccessNetworksForSharedVolumes Cluster parameter as follows:

   (get-cluster -name ClusterName).UseClientAccessNetworksForSharedVolumes = $true

- **Rule 3** SMB Multichannel requires identical link speed and features (RSS and/or RDMA) to stream the CSV redirected traffic over different subnets simultaneously.

- **Rule 4** If adapters are not identical, SMB Multichannel will use the faster adapter/s only to stream the CSV redirected traffic.

- **Rule 5** Failover cluster will fail back to NetFT the decision of what subnet to use only if SMB Multichannel is not available or is disabled. Then the lowest metric logic will apply, and the CSV redirected traffic will be send over the lowest metric subnet.

Rules 1 and 2 indicate that SMB Multichannel is enabled because it is the default configuration in Windows Server 2012, and three network adapters (the internal adapters with role 1) can be used for CSV redirected traffic..

Rules 3 and 4 indicate that Slow network has a slower link speed (100 MB) compared with networks Contoso_Cluster and Live Migration, so this explains why these two cluster networks will be used for CSV redirected traffic.

In some scenarios, you may need to force use only one particular subnet for CSV redirected traffic and avoid SMB Multichannel, even if it's the last recommended step. To achieve that, you must disable SMB Multichannel using the following command:

Set-SMBClientConfiguration -EnableMultichannel $False

Then reboot the server. Note that you must apply this on all cluster nodes. After this change, the cluster will use the NetFT Network Priorities and will be forced to use only the subnet with the lowest metric that you have manually configured.

—*Cristian Edwards Sabathe, EMEA PFE Regional Workload Lead for Server Virtualization*

Additional resources

Here is an additional resource concerning this topic:

- Cluster Shared Volumes Reborn in Windows Server 2012: Deep Dive (Channel 9 PowerPoint slide deck) at:
  http://video.ch9.ms/teched/2012/na/WSV430.pptx

Multitenant networking: Single cluster

Multitenancy is the ability of a cloud infrastructure to support virtual machine workloads of multiple tenants in a secure fashion. With multitenancy, all of the workloads run on the same infrastructure while being isolated from each other. The multiple workloads of each tenant can interconnect with each other and be managed remotely, but they do not interconnect with the workloads of other tenants or be remotely managed by them.

Multitenancy is a key capability built into the Hyper-V role of Windows Server 2012 and is a key ingredient for building cloud computing platforms. Multitenancy can be implemented using Network Virtualization, which provides virtual networks to virtual machines similar to how server virtualization (hypervisor) provides virtual machines to the operating system.

In this section, Jason Dinwiddie, a Senior Consultant with Microsoft Consulting Services, describes in some detail the different scenarios you can use to implement multitenant networking using a single failover cluster of Hyper-V hosts. By choosing the right scenario you can optimize the performance of your environment, provide redundancy against various kinds of network failure, and ensure isolation between tenants.

Scenario overview

Virtualization technologies have provided the ability to reduce hardware footprint and simplify management and provisioning, in addition to a whole host of other benefits. Still, the need remains to provide infrastructure for various environments that provide different arenas for application and system lifecycles. The need for development and testing environments is increasingly important for everything from application development to everyday operations such as patch management and product upgrades.

The following scenario will walk you through the options for isolating and optimizing networks while hosting multiple environments within a single Hyper-V cluster.

The scenario:
- Tenant 1: Development
- Tenant 2: UAT
- Tenant 3: Production
- Single Hyper-V Cluster

Networking Requirements:

- Redundancy: Needs to be resilient to NIC or switch failures
- Communication Isolation: Tenants cannot communicate with each other directly
- Performance: Need predictability of performance at the network level

Option 1: Consolidated network (single NIC team)

Option 1 is a common scenario. With the advent of the 10GbE network, a consolidation of networks into a small number of physical connections is a good solution. In this scenario, a single team of 10GbE NICs will provide network communication to all virtual machines and the host. This scenario requires host-level communication for Live Migration, Cluster, and Host Management.

NOTE Storage connectivity is not included in this discussion.

The following diagram provides a high-level logical view of the host configuration for this scenario and shows a consolidated network with a single team:

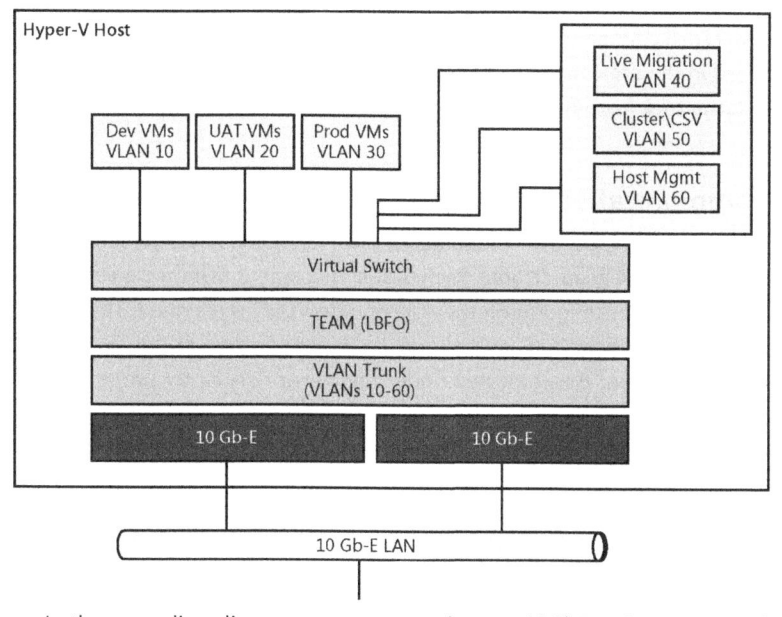

In the preceding diagram, you can see the two 10GbE NICs are teamed using native Windows Server 2012 NIC Teaming (LBFO), and is presented with a VLAN trunk that includes all necessary VLANs. On top of the team a V-Switch is created inside of Hyper-V to which all virtual machines and the host virtual NICs will connect.

Requirement 1: Redundancy

To provide redundancy at the network level, the scenario leverages native Windows Server 2012 NIC Teaming (LBFO). By teaming the adapters, in the event of a NIC, switch port, or switch failure we can prevent any loss of connectivity since the communication will continue through the available link.

> **NOTE** In addition to redundancy, this optimization also helps in the performance requirement. By aggregating the 10GbE links in a single team we can provide 20GbE bandwidth under standard working conditions.

NIC teaming can be managed either inside Server Manager, or via PowerShell.

```
# Create a NIC team that consists of two 10GbE NICs
New-NetLbfoTeam "2x10GbE Team" –TeamMembers "10GbE NIC1","10GbE NIC2" –TeamNicName "2x10GbE"
```

```
# Create a Hyper-V Virtual Switch that binds to the NIC team
New-VMSwitch "20GbE switch" –NetAdapterName "2x10GbE" –MinimumBandwidthMode Weight –AllowManagementOS $false
```

> **NOTE** The above PowerShell command creates a VSwitch inside Hyper-V that is attached to the NIC team created in the previous step. Notice the –MimimumBandwidthMode is set to weight (that is important for Requirement 3 below).

Requirement 2: Communication isolation

To keep the tenants isolated while riding over the same physical network, all VLANs are presented to the single Hyper-V NIC team (trunk). Each virtual machine is assigned a virtual NIC, and inside the virtual machine configuration the appropriate VLAN is assigned. This can be accomplished via the UI by selecting the Enable Virtual LAN Identification option and entering the appropriate VLAN value. This is located under the Network Adapter properties for each virtual machine.

Additionally, this can be accomplished via PowerShell with the following sample command:

```
# Assign VLAN ID to Virtual Machines network adapter
Set-VMNetworkAdapterVlan –VM ["VM Name"] –VMNetworkAdapterName ["VMNetworkadapter Name"] –Access –VlanId 10
```

The above command is used to set the VLAN ID for a Development tenant virtual machine. Once all virtual machines have been configured with a proper virtual NIC and VLAN ID, they will be isolated and unable to communicate with any of the other tenants.

This process needs to be followed for the Host virtual NIC as well but can only be performed via PowerShell.

First create the virtual NIC for the host:

```
# Create a virtual NIC in the management operating system for Live Migration
Add-VMNetworkAdapter –ManagementOS –Name "LM" –SwitchName ["20GbE switch"]
```

Next add the VLAN ID that corresponds with the VNic just created:

```
# Assign a VLAN to the virtual NIC in the management OS for Live Migration
Set-VMNetworkAdapterVlan –ManagementOS –VMNetworkAdapterName LM –Access –VlanId 200
```

Repeat this process for all of the host networks (Host Management, Cluster, CSV, etc.), and then the host communication is isolated to that VLAN.

Requirement 3: Performance

To provide performance predictability and optimize performance in this scenario, a couple of solutions can be implemented. The first is dynamic Virtual Machine Queues (VMQ). VMQ is enabled by default but must be supported by the underlying NICs. This option spreads the network processing across CPUs in the root partition (host) adaptively, using more cores during heavy load and fewer cores during light loads. This optimizes network performance for the virtual machines.

The second solution is Hyper-V QoS (Quality of Service). For each port in the virtual switch both minimum and maximum bandwidth settings can be configured. The maximum value is a ceiling, which tells a machine or host network connection it can never exceed the configured value. The minimum value is a floor, which tells a virtual machine or host network connection that it will never have less than the configured value available to it. These settings can be configured on the fly via PowerShell (see below). Using Hyper-V QoS will provide the predictability of network service and prevent particular tenants from taking over, causing a performance impact to the other tenants.

In the previous sections, we configured the VSwitch and assigned virtual NIC to each virtual machine as well as the host connections. Once the virtual NICs are assigned and the VLAN ID is set, we can configure the QoS settings for each virtual NIC\Port.

Depending on how the VSwitch was configured, either an absolute value or a weight (priority) will be assigned to the virtual machine for minimum bandwidth. Absolute value is measured in bits per second, and weight is a value between 1 and 100.

Here is an example of configuring minimum bandwidth weight:

```
# Assign a weight to Live Migration
Set-VMNetworkAdapter –ManagementOS –Name "LM" –MinimumBandwidthWeight 20

# Assign a weight to a VM as well as a hard cap at 1Gbps
Set-VMNetworkAdapter –VMName ["Vm Name"] -MinimumBandwidthWeight 1 –MaximumBandwidth 1000000000
```

> **NOTE** Configuring a weight is only possible when the switch was created with weight mode.

Option 2: Multiple physical networks (many teams)

In some instances—to use existing hardware assets, to avoid purchasing 10GbE infrastructures, or for other architectural reasons—the solution will require many 1 gigabit NICs and separate physical network connections.

In this scenario, multiple teams are created with network connections attached to a distributed physical layer. The same optimizations and possibilities are achieved at the physical level instead of at the logical level.

NOTE Storage connectivity is not included in this discussion.

The following diagram provides a high-level logical view of the host configuration for this scenario and shows multiple physical networks (many teams):

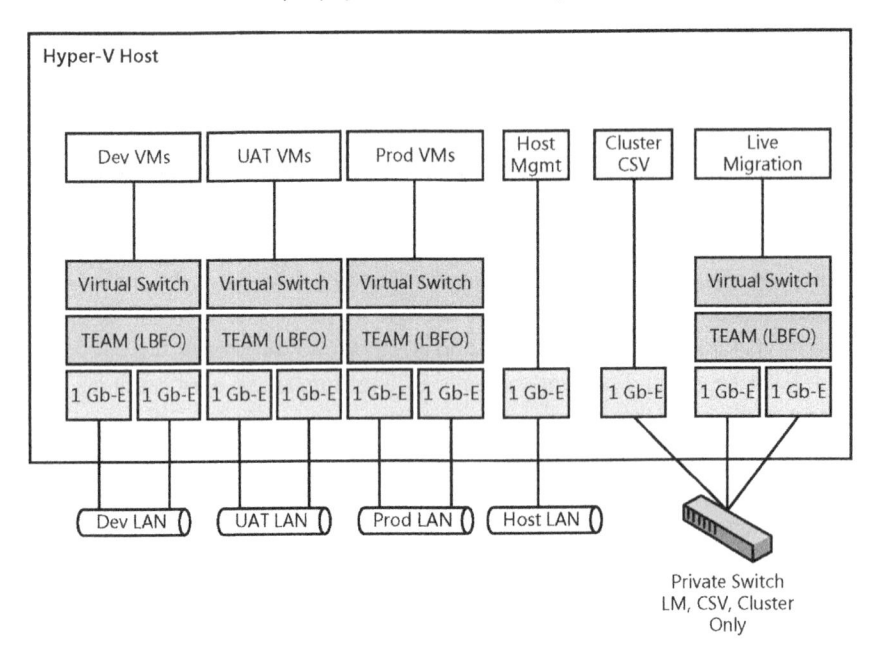

Requirement 1: Redundancy

To provide redundancy at the network level the scenario leverages native Windows Server 2012 NIC Teaming (LBFO). By teaming the adapters, in the event of a NIC, switch port, or switch failure, we can prevent any loss of connectivity since the communication will continue through the available link.

In this case, we would create multiple teams, one for each tenant providing a 2-GB connection. Host Management can be teamed, but in this scenario it is depicted as a single

NIC, no team. Depending on your server hardware capabilities there may be a limit to the number of NICs available.

Requirement 2: Communication isolation

In the first option, to provide communication isolation between the tenants, VLANs were required. That's because they were all riding over a single physical connection. This scenario includes a distributed physical network layer, so the isolation occurs at the physical level and no VLANs are required.

Requirement 3: Performance

Because option 1 sent all traffic over the same physical connection(s), Hyper-V QoS was needed to provide predictable performance to the various tenants and to prevent one tenant from impacting another. Since in this scenario the tenants are split across separate and distinct physical connections, QoS may not be as important. It should be noted that you may still want to use Hyper-V QoS within a tenant to provide the same predictability, but from a network perspective, one tenant can't impact another.

Dynamic VMQ should still be used as stated in option 1 for overall performance gain in network processing speed.

—*Jason Dinwiddie, Senior Consultant with Microsoft Consulting Services*

Additional resources

Here are a few additional resources concerning this topic:
- NIC Teaming Overview (TechNet Library):
  http://technet.microsoft.com/en-us/library/hh831648.aspx
- Network Virtualization technical details (TechNet Library)
  http://technet.microsoft.com/en-us/library/jj134174.aspx

Multitenant networking: IaaS environment

In the previous section, we examined how Windows Server 2012 Hyper-V can be used to implement a solution that provides multitenancy, the ability of a cloud infrastructure to support virtual machine workloads of multiple tenants in a secure fashion. While enterprise customers usually want to build private clouds and transition to an IT-as-a-service operational mode, hosting providers want to build public clouds and offer Infrastructure as a Service (IaaS) solutions to their customers.

In the IaaS model for cloud computing, the service provides servers (typically virtualized), storage, and networks to the customer. The customer then owns the virtual servers and is responsible for maintaining them and installing applications that would otherwise be deployed onto physical servers on premises. Although the IaaS service provider owns all aspects of maintaining the physical infrastructure and using it to the maximum possible, the customer owns the actual workload in the traditional fashion.

In this section, Shabbir Ahmed, a Partner Enterprise Architect with the Partner Enterprise Architect Team, provides some guidance on designing and implementing Hyper-V networking for a multitenant IaaS environment. He examines different scenarios for implementing multitenant isolation, including physical separation and layer 2/3 isolation.

Guidance on Hyper-V networking for a multitenant IaaS environment

Windows Server 2012 running Hyper-V along with the System Center 2012 SP1 suite has been used by many customers and partners to offer multitenant Infrastructure as a Service (IaaS) to their customers. Providing network isolation between tenants in such a way that virtual machines of one tenant cannot communicate with virtual machines of another tenant requires proper design and consideration at the Compute, Hyper-V, and Network (Switches/Firewall) layers.

> **NOTE** This section doesn't address PVLAN, network virtualization, and System Center enhancements concerning virtual networking.

Scenarios

There are three basic ways to achieve isolation between tenants:
- Physical separation
- Layer 2 and Layer 3 isolation
- Network virtualization (not covered in this section)

Physical separation

Physical separation is costly because it requires dedicated switches, routers/firewalls, and NIC cards (and sometimes dedicated servers). The following diagram shows isolated tenants with dedicated physical NIC/server and network devices:

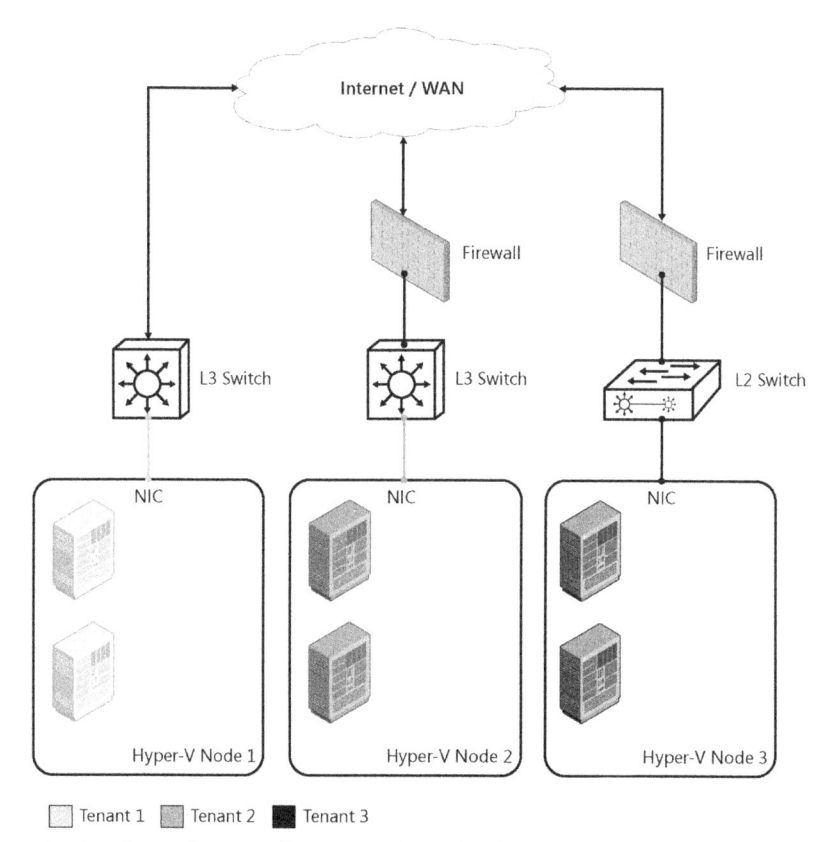

In the above diagram, the tenants have the following dedicated physical resources:
- Tenant 1: NIC/server and Layer 3 switch

    The gateway of the virtual machines is the Layer 3 switch, which is the default route to the Internet.

83

- Tenant 2: NIC/server, Layer 3 switch, and firewall

    The gateway of the virtual machines is the firewall if the Layer 3 switch is running in Layer 2 mode; otherwise the tenant has the option to use either the Layer 3 switch or the firewall as a gateway.

- Tenant 3: NIC/server, Layer 2 switch, and firewall

    The gateway of the virtual machines is the firewall, which is the default route to the Internet.

The physical isolation approach gives customers the flexibility to introduce physical devices of their choice; however, this makes it challenging for the provider to automate end-to-end provisioning.

Providing a dedicated switch and router/firewall provides many options for tenants to extend virtual machine connectivity to physical devices, such as Load Balancer, IPS/IDS devices, and DDOS prevention solutions/services, and also makes high-speed WAN/MPLS termination possible for their respective switches/routers/firewalls.

Physical isolation at the network layer can also be achieved without the use of a dedicated server per tenant. This approach gives the server level high availability at a much lower cost. The following diagram shows isolated tenants with dedicated network devices (and NIC) and shared servers:

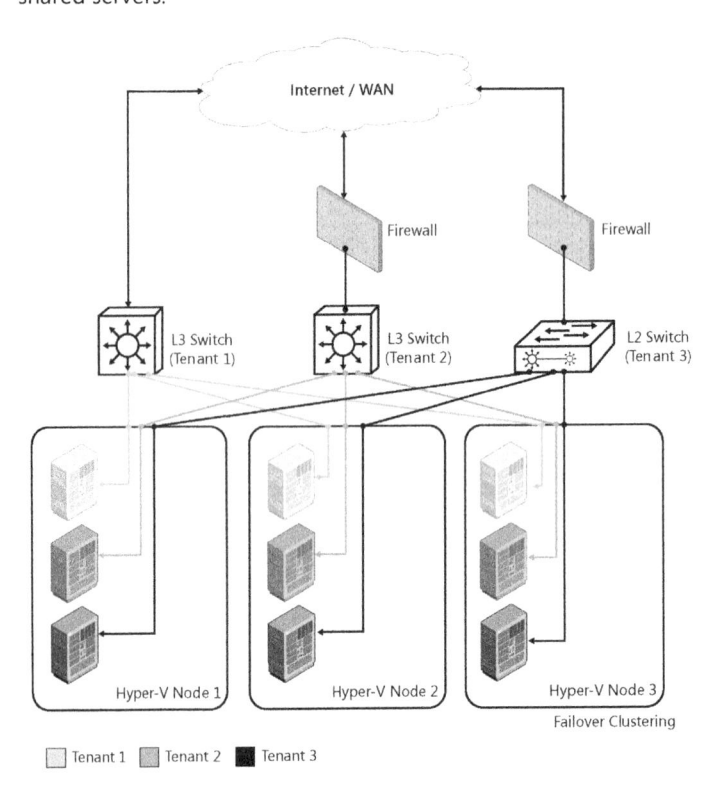

In the above diagram, the server hardware's high availability has been achieved by using failover clustering. For high availability of firewalls/routers, multiple devices can be added, and for switch redundancy, multiple switches can be installed along with multiple NICs (teamed) on each server. We will cover switch redundancy and NIC Teaming later in this section.

Layer 2 and Layer 3 isolation

Although tenant isolation using a physical approach is not complex and provides some benefits, it's a very costly solution and makes providing end-to-end automation challenging when customers want to create and access their virtual machines just by clicking through a few self-service provisioning steps.

System Center 2012 SP1 Virtual Machine Manager along with Windows Server 2012 Hyper-V can provide isolation between tenants through the Network Isolation feature using encapsulation. This approach does not require physical separation or Layer 2 and Layer 3 isolation. However, there are a few scenarios where a provider might prefer Layer 2 and Layer 3 isolation over network virtualization:

- Underlying hardware doesn't support network virtualization.
- Provider needs the tenant's network to be extended to their IaaS's aggregation switch to provide tenants MPLS/WAN termination, and so on, which will communicate to the tenant's virtual machine.

For more details on network virtualization, refer to http://technet.microsoft.com/en-us/library/jj134174.aspx.

Layer 2 isolation is achieved by assigning all the virtual machines of each tenant to a separate VLAN (e.g., VLAN 10 for Tenant 1, VLAN 11 for Tenant 2, etc.), and Layer 3 isolation is achieved by assigning a separate network subnet to the virtual machines of each tenant (e.g., 192.168.1.0/24 for Tenant 1, 192.168.2.0/24 for Tenant 2, etc.).

To use only Layer 2 isolation, a provider can assign the same network subnet (assume 192.168.1.0/24) to multiple tenants. In this case, each tenant's virtual machine gateway should point to a different Layer 3 device (virtual firewall, Layer 3 switch's VLAN, or hardware firewall/router). However, troubleshooting issues in this scenario using a packet capturing tool such as Network Monitor, Wireshark, and so on would display an IP packet of the same address from multiple tenants, which may lead to confusion and delay overall troubleshooting.

In this isolation approach, the network switch's ports that are connected to Hyper-V hosts should be in Trunk mode to pass multiple VLAN traffic. It would be a good idea to allow only those VLANs that are used by tenants from the physical switch's trunk to Hyper-V. Otherwise, if pruning is not configured in the switch, it may lead to an unnecessary broadcast going everywhere. Please refer to the next two diagrams for a high-level view of this isolation approach.

The first diagram shows the Layer 2 and Layer 3 isolation approach for multitenant IaaS (shared firewall and network switch):

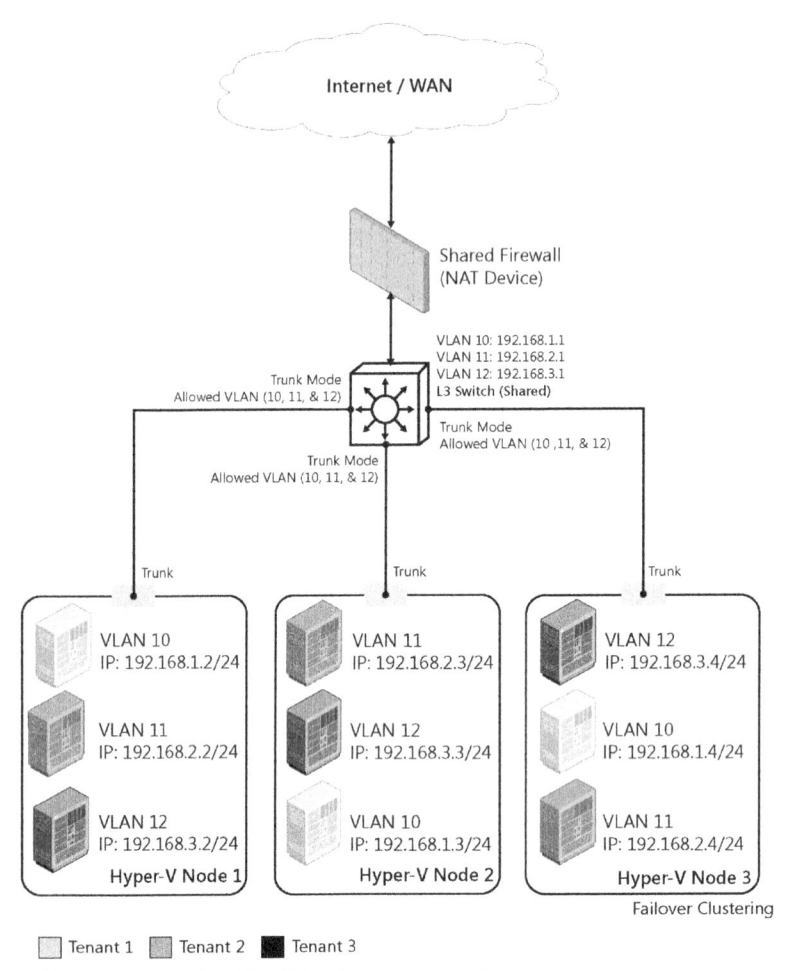

Here are some details of the above approach:

- Tenant 1 is assigned Network subnet 192.168.1.0/24 (L3) and VLAN 10 (L2) by the provider.
- Tenant 2 is assigned Network subnet 192.168.2.0/24 (L3) and VLAN 10 (L2) by the provider.
- Tenant 3 is assigned Network subnet 192.168.3.0/24 (L3) and VLAN 10 (L2) by the provider.
- The gateway address of each tenant's virtual machine is the Layer 3 VLAN IP of the network switch, which further passes the outbound Internet traffic to the firewall.
- The Layer 3 switch is required because routing has to be done on the switch itself.

- The provider bills the tenant/customer for network bandwidth as well as for CPU, memory, and disk usage. Getting the exact Internet bandwidth usage of each tenant is difficult.

The second diagram shows the Layer 3 isolation approach for multitenant IaaS (shared network switch):

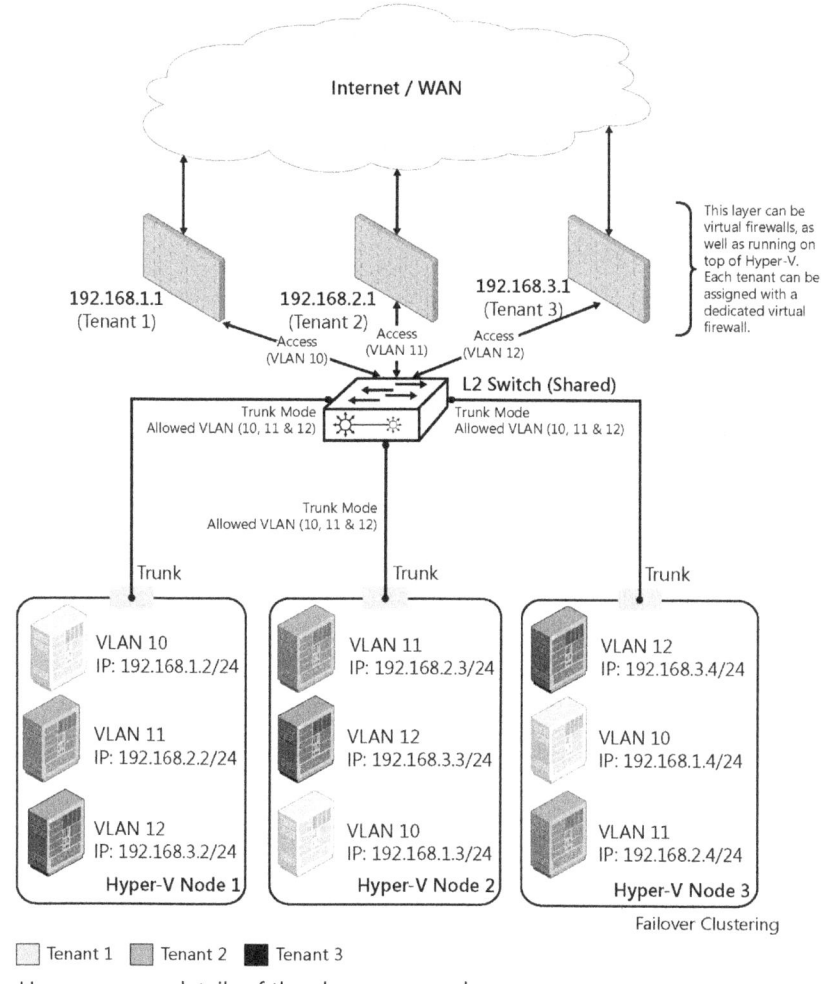

Here are some details of the above approach:

- The Layer 3 switch is optional because the dedicated firewall can do the routing job in addition to providing firewall features.
- The provider can monitor the firewall's internal or external NIC usage to bill the tenant for Internet bandwidth utilization.

- A single firewall with multiple NIC cards can also serve multiple tenants. (However, the tenant should agree to shared firewall usage with another tenant.)
- In the scenario in the figure above, the physical firewall is acting as the tenant's dedicated gateway; however, the provider can use a virtual firewall as well. Vyatta is one of the supported virtual firewalls in Windows Server 2012 Hyper-V. For more information, see http://www.microsoft.com/virtualization/pt/br/partner-detail.aspx?id=114.

Assuming the IaaS design shown above, a provider follows these steps to onboard a new customer/tenant:

1. Plan and assign a VLAN and network subnet to the new tenant (in this example, Tenant 4).
2. Create a VLAN (in this case, 13) on the Layer 3 switch and configure an IP address to act as a gateway for Tenant 4.
3. Allow VLAN 13 on all trunk ports that are connected to the Hyper-V server. (Note: If there are multiple switches for redundancy, VLAN 13 needs to be allowed on those switch ports wherever applicable.) If VLAN is not allowed on all required switch trunk ports that are connected to the Hyper-V host then the virtual machine may lose connectivity when it is live migrated to another host.
4. Create a virtual machine for Tenant 4 on Windows Server 2012 Hyper-V and assign VLAN 13 to all virtual machines of that tenant.
5. Assign an IP address and gateway to the virtual machines.
6. Configure a firewall to allow the virtual machine to be accessed from the Internet. This may involve configuration of NAT, ACLs, and so on.

To automate (for complete self-service) the above onboarding process, a service provider can explore the following options in System Center 2012 SP1:

- Virtual Machine Manager can be used to create virtual machines, assign VLANs, and configure TCP/IP (IP, Gateway, and DNS).
- Virtual Machine Manager can also be used to provision a firewall (virtual firewall such as Vyatta).
- Orchestrator can be used to automate creation of a VLAN on a physical switch, configure trunk-allowed VLAN, assign an IP address to VLAN, create ACL and NAT on firewall, and so on. Note that for this option, the network switch and firewall/router must support SSH. For more information, see http://technet.microsoft.com/en-us/library/hh225041.aspx.

NIC Teaming

NIC Teaming, also known as load balancing and failover (LBFO), allows multiple network adapters on a computer to be placed into a team for the traffic failover to prevent connectivity loss in the event of a network component (Hyper-V NIC or Network Switch) failure or for other purposes.

In earlier versions of Hyper-V, customers were dependent on the NIC card vendor to provide teaming features, and each vendor's logic reacted differently to a virtualization environment. It was always advisable to use updated NIC drivers along with the latest teaming software. Following are links to forum discussions about vendor teaming software that was designed to advertise the Hyper-V host MAC address instead of the actual virtual machine MAC address, which caused virtual machine connectivity loss. (This issue was resolved in the updated version of the teaming software):

- http://social.technet.microsoft.com/Forums/en-US/winserverhyperv/thread/6ff2c285-35fa-4ac6-ba49-7dbe6dc40858
- http://social.technet.microsoft.com/Forums/en-US/winserverhyperv/thread/c4223e6f-65c3-4c59-aa6b-5fb70f0e5abf

NOTE For more detail on the Windows Server 2012 implementation of NIC teaming, refer to http://technet.microsoft.com/en-in/library/hh831648.aspx.

Now it is recommend to use the NIC Teaming feature of Windows Server 2012 instead of the vendor's software, which works beautifully with Hyper-V. The following diagram shows NIC Teaming (failover) with redundant switches:

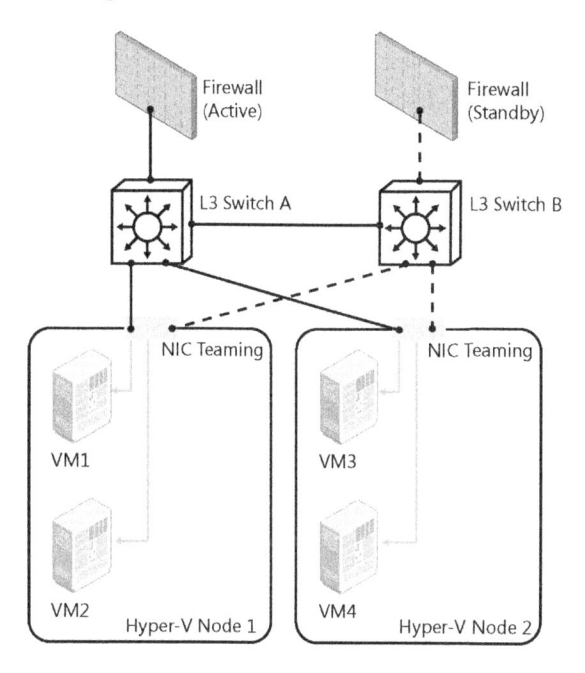

Here are some details of the above approach:

- All the active NICs of teaming are connected to Layer 3 Switch A and all the passive/standby NICs are connected to Layer 3 Switch B. However, it's up to the provider to split active NICs to both of the switches. Many providers prefer to keep all active NICs on one switch because backend throughput of a switch is much higher than connectivity between both the switches. This means will take less time for a virtual machine on Host 1 to reach virtual machines residing in other hosts.

- VLANs that are allowed on a switch trunk port connected to Hyper-V must also be allowed on the trunk port between both of the switches. Otherwise, if the active NIC of Hyper-V Node 1 fails, then the virtual machines residing in both of the hosts would not be able to communicate with each other.

- The firewall's interface that is connected to switch's port would be the access port in most cases. This access port on both switches must be configured with proper VLANs and be allowed in the trunk port between both of the switches.

—*Shabbir Ahmed, Partner Enterprise Architect (Infrastructure) with the Partner Enterprise Architect Team (PEAT)*

Additional resources

Here is an additional resource concerning this topic:
- Hyper-V Network Virtualization Overview (TechNet Library) at: http://technet.microsoft.com/en-us/library/jj134230.aspx

Virtual Machine Queue

Virtual machine queue (VMQ) is a feature available in Hyper-V in Windows Server 2008 R2 and later for hosts that have VMQ-capable network adapters installed on them. VMQ uses hardware packet filtering to deliver packet data from an external virtual machine network directly to virtual machines. This reduces the overhead of routing packets and copying them from the management operating system to the virtual machine.

When VMQ is enabled, a dedicated queue is established on the physical network adapter for each virtual network adapter that has requested a queue. As packets arrive for a virtual network adapter, the physical network adapter places them in that network adapter's queue.

When packets are indicated up, all the packet data in the queue is delivered directly to the virtual network adapter. Network adapter uses DMA (Direct Memory Access) to transfer packets directly to a virtual machine's shared memory.

Packets arriving for virtual network adapters that don't have a dedicated queue, as well as all multicast and broadcast packets, are delivered to the virtual network in the default queue. The virtual network handles routing of these packets to the appropriate virtual network adapters as it normally would.

In this section, Thomas Roettinger, a Program Manager with the Partner and Customer Ecosystem Team, examines a troubleshooting scenario involving running out of virtual machine queues.

Example: Running out of virtual machine queues

Patricia is an administrator who works for a hoster. While onboarding a new tenant, she discovers an error event entry in the system log.

Event ID 113

Source: Hyper-V-VmSwitch

Failed to allocate VMQ for NIC ....(Friendly Name: Network Adapter) on switch ...(Friendly Name: Virtual Switch). Reason - Maximum number of VMQs supported on the Protocol NIC is exceeded. Status = Insufficient system resources exist to complete the API

By running the following PowerShell command, Patricia wants to determine the maximum number of virtual machine queues provided by the physical network card. The information is provided by the network card driver to Windows.

gwmi –Namespace "root\virtualization\v2" –Class Msvm_VirtualEthernetSwitch | select elementname, MaxVMQOffloads

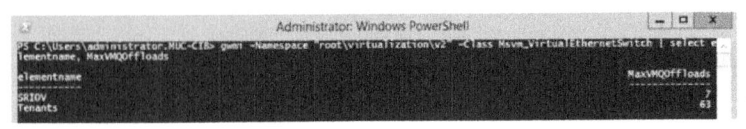

The output shows that the physical network card used by the virtual switch called *Tenant* offers 63 virtual machine queues. This information can be verified by opening the device driver properties, as shown in the following screenshot:

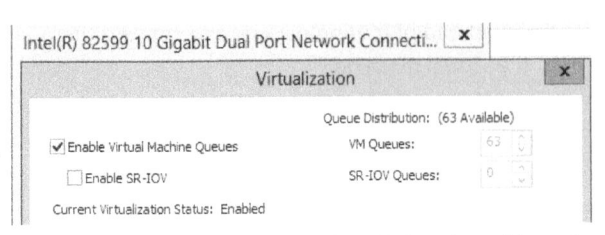

Patricia needs to generate a list of virtual machines that have VMQ enabled to determine which ones require VMQ and which ones do not.

She runs the following PowerShell command:

Get-VM | Get-VMNetworkAdapter | ft name,vmqusage

She also counts the virtual machines on the host to determine how many virtual machines are using VMQ:

Get-VM | Get-VMNetworkAdapter | ft name,vmqusage|measure

After VMQ is disabled for some nodes, the event id is no longer posted to the system event log.

NOTE Another way to resolve this issue is to swap the network cards for a different model that provides more virtual machine queues, or to add additional network cards and create an additional virtual switch.

—*Thomas Roettinger, Program Manager, Partner and Customer Ecosystem Team*

Additional resources

Here is an additional resource concerning this topic:

- Using Virtual Machine Queue (TechNet Library) at: http://technet.microsoft.com/en-us/library/gg162704(v=ws.10).aspx

Hyper-V Replica

Hyper-V Replica is a new feature of Windows Server 2012 that provides asynchronous replication of virtual machines between two Hyper-V hosts. Hyper-V Replica is easy to configure and does not require either shared storage or any particular storage hardware. Any server workload that can be virtualized in Hyper-V can be replicated.

Replication works over any ordinary IP-based network, and the replicated data can be encrypted during transmission. Hyper-V Replica works with standalone servers, failover clusters, or a mixture of both. The servers can be physically co-located or widely separated geographically. The physical servers do not need to be in the same domain, or even joined to any domain at all.

In this section, Mark Ghazai, a Data Center Specialist with the Microsoft U.S. State and Local Government group, demonstrates how to troubleshoot network replication issues in an environment where Hyper-V Replica has been set up.

Hyper-V Replica configuration troubleshooting

Windows Server 2012 Hyper-V Replica is one of the new groundbreaking features of the Microsoft hypervisor that enables a virtual machine to be securely replicated to another Windows Server 2012 Hyper-V host even outside the trusted domain (secured by digital certificates). This exciting feature is a network and storage agnostic that can be configured per virtual machine and also provides replication to VSS (Volume Shadow Copy) aware applications running inside that virtual machine.

Windows Server Hyper-V 2012 Replica overview and deployment considerations can be found in the following TechNet article: http://technet.microsoft.com/en-us/library/jj134172.aspx.

Assuming you have already taken care of the Replication Configuration setting in all the Hyper-V host Hyper-V Settings consoles of all Hyper-V hosts engaged in this transaction, the first issue that you might experience is a failure to enable replication. In this case, you'll notice a longer than usual delay when you try to enable the replica for a virtual machine, and then the following error message will appear:

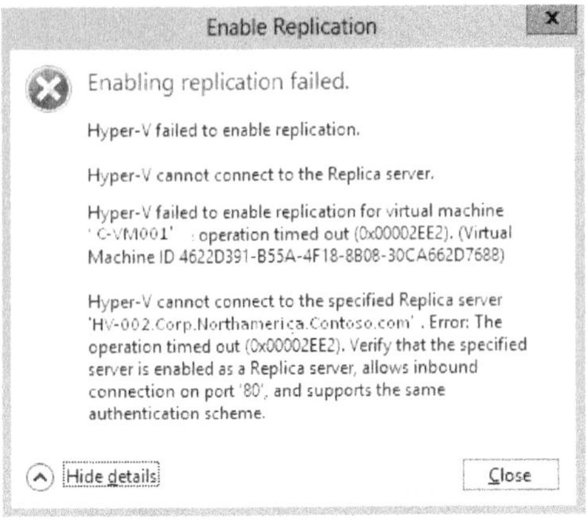
Enable Replication
Enabling replication failed.
Hyper-V failed to enable replication.
Hyper-V cannot connect to the Replica server.
Hyper-V failed to enable replication for virtual machine 'C-VM001' : operation timed out (0x00002EE2). (Virtual Machine ID 4622D391-B55A-4F18-8B08-30CA662D7688)
Hyper-V cannot connect to the specified Replica server 'HV-002.Corp.Northamerica.Contoso.com' . Error: The operation timed out (0x00002EE2). Verify that the specified server is enabled as a Replica server, allows inbound connection on port '80', and supports the same authentication scheme.
Hide details
Close

As the error indicates, this is most likely a connectivity issue. It turns out that the root cause lies on the firewall configuration settings on the receiving end. In this case, the destination Hyper-V server's Windows firewall settings reveal that the Hyper-V Replica HTTP (or HTTPS, if selected) inbound rule is disabled.

The following screenshot shows the Windows Firewall With Advanced Security console:

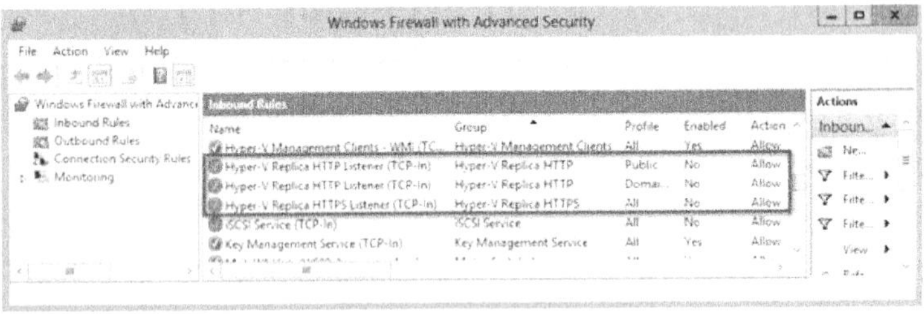
Windows Firewall with Advanced Security
File Action View Help
Inbound Rules
Outbound Rules
Connection Security Rules
Monitoring
Name
Group
Profile
Enabled
Action
Hyper-V Replica HTTP Listener (TCP-In)
Hyper-V Replica HTTP
Hyper-V Replica HTTPS Listener (TCP-In)
Hyper-V Replica HTTPS
iSCSI Service (TCP-In)
iSCSI Service
Key Management Service (TCP-In)
Key Management Service
Actions

You also can find the same settings within the Windows Firewall console under the Windows Control Panel:

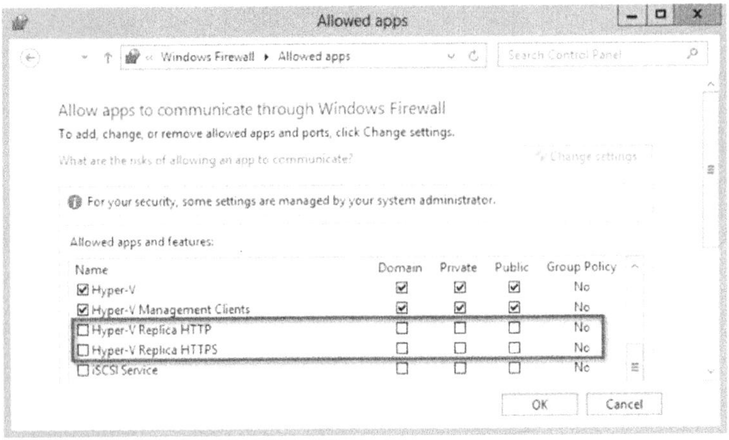
Allowed apps
Windows Firewall ▸ Allowed apps
Search Control Panel
Allow apps to communicate through Windows Firewall
To add, change, or remove allowed apps and ports, click Change settings.
What are the risks of allowing an app to communicate?
Change settings
For your security, some settings are managed by your system administrator.
Allowed apps and features:
Name
Domain
Private
Public
Group Policy
Hyper-V
Hyper-V Management Clients
Hyper-V Replica HTTP
Hyper-V Replica HTTPS
iSCSI Service
No
OK
Cancel

Keep in mind that if those Hyper-V hosts are being managed by Active Directory or Local Group Policy, these settings might need to be added to the active GPO and refreshed on those Hyper-V servers:

Additional troubleshooting steps

I worked with customer who had an exception anytime he attempted to enable the Replica feature. We did some troubleshooting and drove that issue to resolution as I will share below. At the same time, I found out that my PFE friend Dave Guenthner also got to the same resolution for a customer he was working with. He even blogged about this issue on his TechNet blog at http://blogs.technet.com/b/davguents_blog/.

In the scenario I will describe here, the customer's environment was fairly straightforward with domain-joined Windows Server 2012 Hyper-V hosts that were also located in the same datacenter and subnet with gigabit connectivity.

For the sake of consistency and to protect the customer's confidential environment, in this presentation I will use the same configuration my friend Dave used to reproduce this issue in his lab:

- Domain Name: REPLICADOMAIN
- Domain Controller: REPLICADC
- Hyper-V Hosts: REPLICAHOST1 (Primary), REPLICAHOST2 (Replica)

When trying to enable replication for a virtual machine, the customer always received this error:

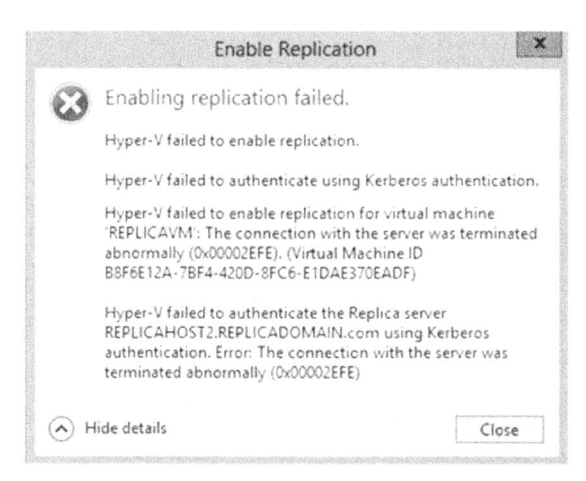

NOTE Hyper-V Replica uses mutual authentication based on Kerberos or mutual authentication based on certificates for the server (not for the user).

As usual, we looked at Windows event logs as the starting point for our troubleshooting. The following event logs and event channels are where I normally start troubleshooting common Hyper-V issues:

- System
- Application
- Security
- Microsoft-Windows-Hyper-V-VMMS

In this case, the following errors appeared in the Microsoft-Windows-Hyper-V-VMMS event channel:

02/04/2013 01:12:06 PM   Error   ITSUSRALAB039.df 32000   Microsoft-Windows-Hyper-V-VMMS   N/A   NT AUTHORITY\SYSTEM   Hyper-V failed to enable replication for virtual machine 'YOURVMNAME': The connection with the server was terminated abnormally (0x00002EFE).

02/01/2013 03:35:17 PM   Error   ITSUSRALAB039.df 29212   Microsoft-Windows-Hyper-V-VMMS   N/A   NT AUTHORITY\SYSTEM   Hyper-V failed to authenticate the primary server using Kerberos authentication. Error: The logon attempt failed (0x8009030C).

TIP You can use the Microsoft Exchange Server Error Code Look-up tool (ERR.exe) found at http://www.microsoft.com/en-us/download/details.aspx?id=985 to help convert the error codes to text.

The most interesting error was this one:

Err.exe 0x8009030C
for hex 0x8009030c / decimal -2146893044
  SEC_E_LOGON_DENIED   winerror.h

This pointed to a logon error. After looking into security logs and discussing this with the customer, I discovered that they had a security template for servers and that they had removed most default user groups from the Access This Computer From The Network policy. The user experiencing the replication issue wasn't part of allowed groups on the Hyper-V servers.

Adding an appropriate group of users to the local security policy resolved this issue:

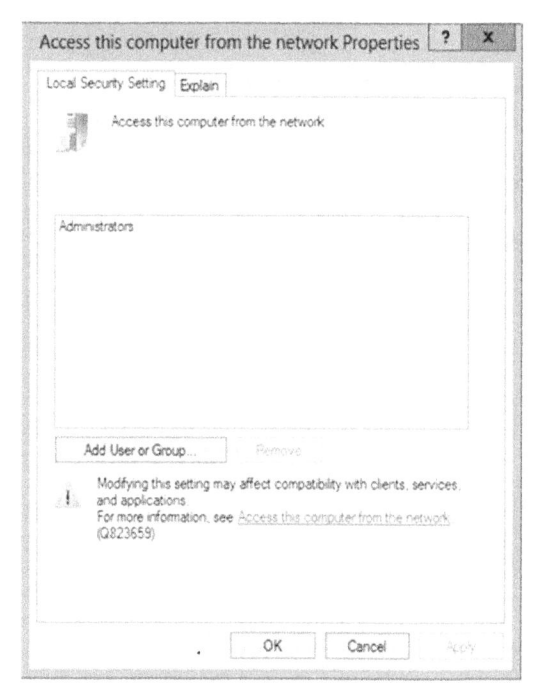

Now, Dave took few more steps when troubleshooting this issue that could be very useful for other possible issues. Below are those extra steps.

NOTE Each command would need to be executed against each Hyper-V host's computer account.

The deployment guide provides specific guidance on what is required for Kerberos delegation, and this seems like a reasonable place to start, along with verifying that all the SPNs are registered. There are a couple of ways to verify this information. One would be to use ldifde.exe to dump all the configuration settings of the computer object in Active Directory. The command using ldifde.exe would look this:

C:\>ldifde -d "CN=REPLICAHOST1,CN=Computers,DC=REPLICADOMAIN,DC=com" -f REPLICAHOST1.log
Connecting to "REPLICADC.REPLICADOMAIN.com"
Logging in as current user using SSPI
Exporting directory to file output.log
Searching for entries...
Writing out entries..
2 entries exported
The command has completed successfully

97

To retrieve the SPNs for each computer object, you can leverage setspn.exe. The command would be:

C:\>setspn -L REPLICADOMAIN\REPLICAHOST1

Registered ServicePrincipalNames for CN=REPLICAHOST1,CN=Computers,DC=REPLICADOMAIN,DC=com:

Hyper-V Replica Service/REPLICAHOST1
Hyper-V Replica Service/REPLICAHOST1.REPLICADOMAIN.com
Microsoft Virtual System Migration Service/REPLICAHOST1
Microsoft Virtual System Migration Service/REPLICAHOST1.REPLICADOMAIN.com
Microsoft Virtual Console Service/REPLICAHOST1
Microsoft Virtual Console Service/REPLICAHOST1.REPLICADOMAIN.com
WSMAN/REPLICAHOST1
WSMAN/REPLICAHOST1.REPLICADOMAIN.com
TERMSRV/REPLICAHOST1
TERMSRV/REPLICAHOST1.REPLICADOMAIN.com
HOST/REPLICAHOST1
HOST/REPLICAHOST1.REPLICADOMAIN.com

Next, verify that the computer objects have Kerberos delegated correctly:

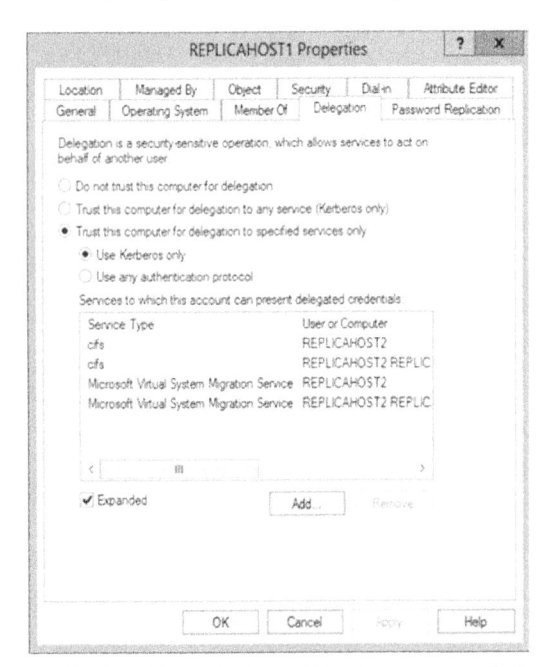

Next, verify each Hyper-V host can successfully communicate with Active Directory:

C:\>nltest /SC_VERIFY:REPLICADOMAIN

Flags: b0 HAS_IP HAS_TIMESERV

Trusted DC Name \\REPLICADC.REPLICADOMAIN.com

Trusted DC Connection Status Status = 0 0x0 NERR_Success

Trust Verification Status = 0 0x0 NERR_Success

The command completed successfully

Verify that KDC is assigning Kerberos tickets:

C:>klist

Current LogonId is 0:0x3364e

Cached Tickets: (7)

#0> Client: Administrator @ REPLICADOMAIN.COM

Server: krbtgt/REPLICADOMAIN.COM @ REPLICADOMAIN.COM

KerbTicket Encryption Type: AES-256-CTS-HMAC-SHA1-96

Ticket Flags 0x60a10000 -> forwardable forwarded renewable pre_authent name_canonicalize

Start Time: 2/6/2013 15:38:20 (local)

End Time: 2/7/2013 0:36:21 (local)

Renew Time: 2/13/2013 14:36:21 (local)

Session Key Type: AES-256-CTS-HMAC-SHA1-96

Cache Flags: 0x2 -> DELEGATION

Kdc Called: REPLICADC.REPLICADOMAIN.com

#1> Client: Administrator @ REPLICADOMAIN.COM

Server: krbtgt/REPLICADOMAIN.COM @ REPLICADOMAIN.COM

KerbTicket Encryption Type: AES-256-CTS-HMAC-SHA1-96

Ticket Flags 0x40e10000 -> forwardable renewable initial pre_authent name_canonicalize

Start Time: 2/6/2013 14:36:21 (local)

End Time: 2/7/2013 0:36:21 (local)

Renew Time: 2/13/2013 14:36:21 (local)

Session Key Type: AES-256-CTS-HMAC-SHA1-96

Cache Flags: 0x1 -> PRIMARY

Kdc Called: REPLICADC.REPLICADOMAIN.com

#2> Client: Administrator @ REPLICADOMAIN.COM

Server: cifs/REPLICADC.REPLICADOMAIN.com @ REPLICADOMAIN.COM

KerbTicket Encryption Type: AES-256-CTS-HMAC-SHA1-96

Ticket Flags 0x40a50000 -> forwardable renewable pre_authent ok_as_delegate name_canonicalize

Start Time: 2/6/2013 15:38:20 (local)

End Time: 2/7/2013 0:36:21 (local)

Renew Time: 2/13/2013 14:36:21 (local)

Session Key Type: AES-256-CTS-HMAC-SHA1-96

Cache Flags: 0

Kdc Called: REPLICADC.REPLICADOMAIN.com

#3> Client: Administrator @ REPLICADOMAIN.COM

Server: ldap/REPLICADC.REPLICADOMAIN.com @ REPLICADOMAIN.COM

KerbTicket Encryption Type: AES-256-CTS-HMAC-SHA1-96

Ticket Flags 0x40a50000 -> forwardable renewable pre_authent ok_as_delegate name_canonicalize

Start Time: 2/6/2013 15:38:20 (local)

End Time: 2/7/2013 0:36:21 (local)
Renew Time: 2/13/2013 14:36:21 (local)
Session Key Type: AES-256-CTS-HMAC-SHA1-96
Cache Flags: 0
Kdc Called: REPLICADC.REPLICADOMAIN.com

#4> Client: Administrator @ REPLICADOMAIN.COM
Server: RPCSS/REPLICAHOST2 @ REPLICADOMAIN.COM
KerbTicket Encryption Type: AES-256-CTS-HMAC-SHA1-96
Ticket Flags 0x40a10000 -> forwardable renewable pre_authent name_canonicalize
Start Time: 2/6/2013 14:39:01 (local)
End Time: 2/7/2013 0:36:21 (local)
Renew Time: 2/13/2013 14:36:21 (local)
Session Key Type: AES-256-CTS-HMAC-SHA1-96
Cache Flags: 0
Kdc Called: REPLICADC.REPLICADOMAIN.com

#5> Client: Administrator @ REPLICADOMAIN.COM
Server: LDAP/REPLICADC.REPLICADOMAIN.com/REPLICADOMAIN.com @ REPLICADOMAIN.COM
KerbTicket Encryption Type: AES-256-CTS-HMAC-SHA1-96
Ticket Flags 0x40a50000 -> forwardable renewable pre_authent ok_as_delegate name_canonicalize
Start Time: 2/6/2013 14:36:53 (local)
End Time: 2/7/2013 0:36:21 (local)
Renew Time: 2/13/2013 14:36:21 (local)
Session Key Type: AES-256-CTS-HMAC-SHA1-96
Cache Flags: 0
Kdc Called: REPLICADC.REPLICADOMAIN.com

#6> Client: Administrator @ REPLICADOMAIN.COM
Server: RPCSS/REPLICAHOST2.REPLICADOMAIN.com @ REPLICADOMAIN.COM
KerbTicket Encryption Type: AES-256-CTS-HMAC-SHA1-96
Ticket Flags 0x40a10000 -> forwardable renewable pre_authent name_canonicalize
Start Time: 2/6/2013 14:36:21 (local)
End Time: 2/7/2013 0:36:21 (local)
Renew Time: 2/13/2013 14:36:21 (local)
Session Key Type: AES-256-CTS-HMAC-SHA1-96
Cache Flags: 0
Kdc Called: REPLICADC.REPLICADOMAIN.com

So far everything looks good in our example; no indications of a Kerberos problem. At this point, we move on to running a network trace from the Primary and Replica servers simultaneously. In previous versions of Windows, we would need to install Netmon or Wireshark to collect this information. A really great trick is leveraging ETW providers to collect the trace.

Here are the commands to start the trace:

ipconfig /flushdns
klist purge
netsh trace start capture = yes
repro issue

Here is the command to stop the trace:

netsh trace stop

You can then copy the ETL trace files to your local machine and view them with Netmon. Unfortunately, in our case, the network trace reveals no clues on where to look next.

When in doubt, always turn to Process Monitor (you can get it from http://live.sysinternals.com) and collect a trace on both sides. In our scenario, doing so didn't reveal any Access_Denied or anything else of interest.

At this point, I decided to refocus on the error itself...Kerberos. I enabled Kerberos debug logging on each Hyper-V machine, reproduced the issue, and then stopped trace. Here is the command to start the trace:

Logman.exe start kerb -p "Security: Kerberos Authentication" 0x40043 -o .\kerb.etl -ets

Run through the Hyper-V wizard and stop traces immediately when the exception is raised. Stop the trace using this command:

Logman.exe stop kerb –ets

Rename Kerb.etl to include the respective server name from both servers. Unfortunately, in order to convert this trace, you will need to engage CTS Support. My trace revealed a clue that really helped:

Failed to create token: 0xc000015b. Let's convert that:
err.exe 0xc000015b
STATUS_LOGON_TYPE_NOT_GRANTED

To me, this has more to do with user rights security rather than Kerberos security. In comparing user rights assignments between two environments, I noticed a difference that would lead to a break in the case. From the Local Group Policy Editor, here are the differences. First, here is the working scenario using the default settings for Windows:

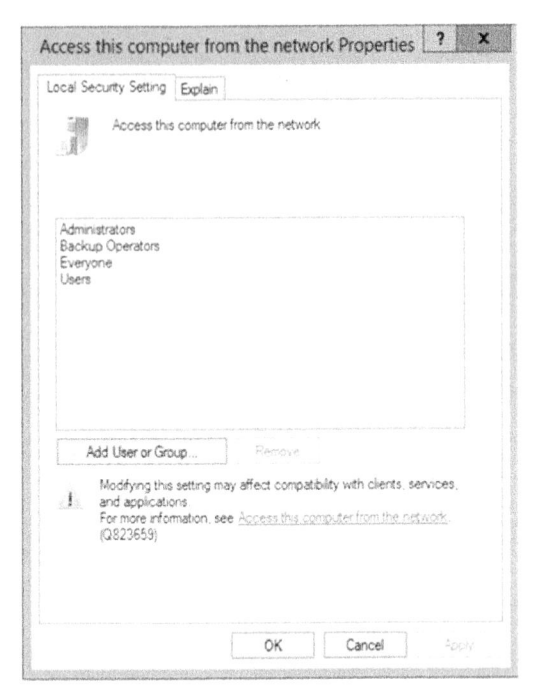

Now here is the broken scenario from the customer environment:

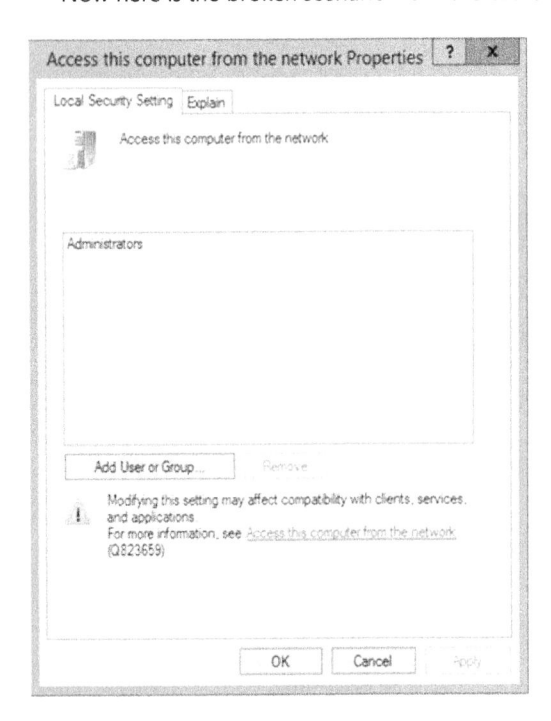

Now we are getting somewhere! If this is a security issue, shouldn't an event have been written to the security log that I reviewed in the beginning? Yes. I simply missed it because I only looked at the security log on the primary machine, not the replica. Going back to the security log, I found the following event on the replica server:

Log Name: Security
Source: Microsoft-Windows-Security-Auditing
Date: 2/6/2013 12:02:01 PM
Event ID: 4625
Task Category: Logon
Level: Information
Keywords: Audit Failure
User: N/A
Computer: REPLICAHOST2.REPLICADOMAIN.com
Description:
An account failed to log on.
Subject:
 Security ID: NULL SID
 Account Name: -
 Account Domain: -
 Logon ID: 0x0
 Logon Type: 3
 Account For Which Logon Failed:
 Security ID: NULL SID
 Account Name: REPLICAHOST1$
 Account Domain: REPLICADOMAIN.COM
 Failure Information:
 Failure Reason: The user has not been granted the requested logon type at this machine.
 Status: 0xC000015B
 Sub Status: 0x0
 Process Information:
 Caller Process ID: 0x0
 Caller Process Name: -
 Network Information:
 Workstation Name: -
 Source Network Address: -
 Source Port: -
 Detailed Authentication Information:
 Logon Process: Kerberos
 Authentication Package: Kerberos
 Transited Services: -
 Package Name (NTLM only): -
 Key Length: 0

Note the following line from the above output:

Failure Reason: The user has not been granted the requested logon type at this machine.

It ended up that Dave's customer also had a requirement to harden Windows security where possible, so instead of simply adding back in all the Windows defaults, they granted Authenticated Users group the user right Access This Computer From The Network on both machines, which resolved the issue for them as well.

—*Mark Ghazai, Data Center Specialist, Microsoft U.S. State and Local Government (SLG)*

Additional resources

Here is an additional resource concerning this topic:

- Hyper-V Replica Overview (TechNet Library) at: http://technet.microsoft.com/en-us/library/jj134172.aspx

Network Virtualization

Network Virtualization is a new feature of Hyper-V in Windows Server 2012 that provides the concept of a virtual network that is independent of the underlying physical network. Network Virtualization does this by providing virtual networks to virtual machines similar to how server virtualization (hypervisor) provides virtual machines to the operating system.

Network Virtualization decouples virtual networks from the physical network infrastructure and removes the constraints of VLAN and hierarchical IP address assignment from virtual machine provisioning. This flexibility makes it easy for customers to move to IaaS clouds and efficient for hosters and datacenter administrators to manage their infrastructure, while maintaining the necessary multitenant isolation and security requirements, and supporting overlapping virtual machine IP addresses.

Because Network Virtualization decouples a business unit's virtual network topology from the actual physical network topology, it provides flexibility and efficiency for private clouds. This means that different business units in an organization can easily share an internal private cloud while being isolated from each other. The datacenter operations team then has the flexibility to deploy and dynamically move workloads anywhere in the datacenter without server interruptions, providing better operational efficiencies and an overall more effective datacenter.

While Network Virtualization can be implemented and managed using only Windows PowerShell, an easier approach is to use System Center Virtual Machine Manager (VMM) 2012 Service Pack 1.

This section has guidance provided by two individuals working at Microsoft. First, Nick Eales, a Senior Premier Field Engineer, demonstrates how to troubleshoot an issue involving two virtual machines that can't communicate even though they are on different hosts but on the same virtual machine network. Then Tim Quinn, a Support Escalation Engineer, goes into detail concerning tracing the VMM Network Virtualization components.

Troubleshooting why two virtual machines on the same virtual machine network but different hosts can't communicate

When using System Center Virtual Machine Manager (SCVMM) to manage Network Virtualization, if SCVMM loses connection with the hosts, or if a configuration mistake is made within SCVMM, it is possible for virtual machines to be unable to communicate.

Troubleshooting using the native Hyper-V PowerShell commands can help with understanding how Network Virtualization works and can identify where configuration issues (if any) exist within SCVMM.

For the purposes of this section, we will be troubleshooting why the virtual machines VM1 and VM4 cannot communicate as per this design diagram below:

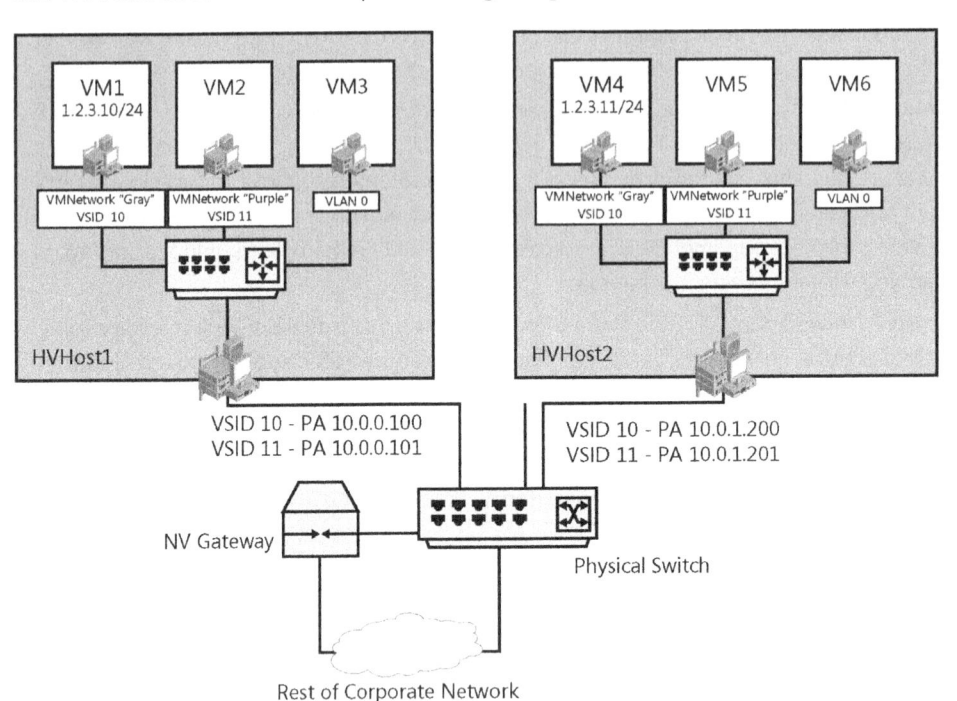

The high level steps we will follow are (the detail is provided later):

1. Check that each virtual machine has the same VirtualSubnetId.
2. Check that the lookup records are correct on each host for the virtual machines. The lookup records identify which host to send the network traffic to for each virtual machine.
3. Check that a WNV subnet gateway address exists on each host for the virtual machines.
4. Check that a WNV route exists on each host for each subnet in the virtual machine network.
5. Check that each virtual machine's host has the same provider address that was specified in the lookup records.
6. Check that the provider routes are correct on each host (this may be empty if the provider addresses are in the same subnet).
7. Check that each host has Network Virtualization bound to a network adapter.

NOTE Very little of the below information or troubleshooting steps are displayed or can be performed using the native Windows graphical user interface (GUI). As of the time of writing, PowerShell and WMI are the only methods available to collect the needed information. PowerShell is used in the below examples because it is easily put into a script and should be familiar to most Windows administrators.

Step 1: Check that each virtual machine has the same VirtualSubnetId

For virtual machines to communicate, they need to be part of the same virtual machine network (in Hyper-V, these are identified by a VirtualSubnetId) or have a Network Virtualization gateway device to be able to route between them.

The native Hyper-V PowerShell command Get-VMNetworkAdapter is used to identify the VirtualSubnetID for the virtual machines. The information that we want from this command should be specified (using the format-table or format-list commands). For example:

PS C:\> Get-VMNetworkAdapter -computer hvhost1 -all | format-table vmname,macaddress,virtualsubnetid,status,ipaddresses -autosize

VMName	MacAddress	VirtualSubnetId	Status	IPAddresses
	00155D968502	0	{Ok}	
VM1	00155D968500	10	{Ok}	{192.168.1.10}
VM2	00155D967D06	11	{Ok}	{172.16.0.10}
VM3	00155D96850B	0	{Degraded,ProtocolVersion}	{}

PS C:\> Get-VMNetworkAdapter -computer hvhost2 -all | format-table vmname,macaddress,virtualsubnetid,status,ipaddresses -autosize

VMName	MacAddress	VirtualSubnetId	Status	IPAddresses
	00155D968503	0	{Ok}	
VM4	00155D968501	10	{Ok}	{192.168.1.11}
VM5	00155D967D07	11	{Ok}	{172.16.0.11}
VM6	00155D96850C	0	{Degraded,ProtocolVersion}	{}

In the above output, we see:

- The virtual machines we are interested in (VM1 and VM4) have the same virtual subnet ID.
- The first line of each output (with no virtual machine name) is for the virtual adapter connected to the host OS (we can ignore this line).
- VM3 and VM6 have out-of-date integration components, and one of the effects in this case is that we don't get an IP address from those virtual machines.

107

- VM3, VM6, and the host virtual adapters have a virtual subnet ID of zero (0), indicating that they are not connected to a virtual machine network in the Network Virtualization space.
- All the MAC addresses are unique. SCVMM will try to ensure that MAC addresses are unique, and this works well provided that the Hyper-V console is not used to add virtual machines or network adapters to virtual machines.

Note that a virtual machine can either have a VirtualSubnetId or a VLAN, not both (the value for either is 0 when not being used).

The VirtualSubnetId of a virtual machine is represented in SCVMM as a VM Subnet that a virtual machine is connected to. The virtual subnet ID of a virtual machine can be displayed using this command:

(Get-SCVirtualNetworkAdapter -vm "VMName").vmnetwork.vmsubnet.VMSubnetID

Step 2: Check that the lookup records are correct on each host for the virtual machines

The lookup records identify which host to send the network traffic to for each virtual machine. These lookup records supply the provider address of the host for each WNV virtual machine's virtual network adapter. This information tells each host where to send the traffic for each virtual machine. Each host stores an independent copy of all of these records. Each host needs its lookup record table to be updated each time a virtual machine is moved, created, or deleted. For routing purposes, the MAC address in this table is what is used to identify the destination. Typically SCVMM builds and maintains this table.

The command to display the lookup records is Get-NetVirtualizationLookupRecord:

PS C:\> Get-NetVirtualizationLookupRecord -CIMSession "HVHost1" | sort VMName | ft
PSComputerName,VMName,MacAddress,VirtualSubnetID,CustomerAddress,ProviderAddress –AutoSize

PSComputerName	VMName	MacAddress	VirtualSubnetID	CustomerAddress	ProviderAddress
HVHost1	GW	005056000000	10	192.168.1.1	1.1.1.1
HVHost1	GW	005056000001	11	172.16.0.1	1.1.1.1
HVHost1	VM1	00155D968500	10	192.168.1.10	10.0.0.100
HVHost1	VM2	00155D967D06	11	172.16.0.10	10.0.0.101
HVHost1	VM4	00155D968501	10	192.168.1.11	10.0.1.200
HVHost1	VM5	00155D967D07	11	172.16.0.11	10.0.1.201

PS C:\> Get-NetVirtualizationLookupRecord -CIMSession "HVHost2" | sort VMName | ft
PSComputerName,VMName,MacAddress,VirtualSubnetID,CustomerAddress,ProviderAddress –AutoSize

PSComputerName VMName MacAddress VirtualSubnetID CustomerAddress ProviderAddress
-------------- ------ ---------- --------------- --------------- ---------------

HVHost2	GW	005056000002	10 192.168.1.1	1.1.1.1	
HVHost2	GW	005056000003	11 172.16.0.1	1.1.1.1	
HVHost2	VM1	00155D968500	10 192.168.1.10	10.0.0.100	
HVHost2	VM2	00155D967D06	11 172.16.0.10	10.0.0.101	
HVHost2	VM4	00155D968501	10 192.168.1.11	10.0.1.200	
HVHost2	VM5	00155D967D07	11 172.16.0.11	10.0.1.201	

In the above output, notice the following:

- The virtualization lookup records for all virtual machines are identical on all hosts. (Ignore the "GW" records for now—they are explained in the next step.)
- The customer address matches the virtual machine's IP address settings.
- The record information for the host name, MACAddress, and VirtualSubnetID match what was displayed for each virtual machine in step 1.
- The PSComputerName field is the machine hosting the lookup record, not the machine that the provider address refers to.

Step 3: Check that a WNV subnet gateway address exists on each host for the virtual machines

These gateway addresses are created by SCVMM and are needed for any routing between subnets within a virtual machine network, and are also required for communication to leave the virtual network.

The information for this was displayed in the previous step, using the command Get-NetVirtualizationLookupRecord.

In this output, look for the following:

- The "GW" record is present on both host machines, and there is a record for each VirtualSubnetID on each host..
- No virtual machines are using the reserved IP address for the subnet gateway (the ".1" of each subnet).
- The MAC addresses of the gateway records are unique (for each virtual subnet, across all hosts).
- The provider addresses for these records do not refer to any physical machines, and can be ignored.

The text *GW* is assigned by SCVMM and so should read the same in most environments. The text itself is unimportant. What is important is that the MAC address is unique on all hosts and does not refer to any virtual machines and that the IP address is not used by anything else.

Step 4: Check that a WNV route exists on each host for each subnet in the virtual machine network

These customer routes provide the information to route between subnets within a virtual machine network and also to route in and out of the Network Virtualization environment.

The command to display the customer routes is get-NetVirtualizationCustomerRoute:

PS C:\> get-NetVirtualizationCustomerRoute -cimsession "HVHost1"| sort VirtualSubnetId,PSComputerName,DestinationPrefix | ft PSComputerName,VirtualSubnetID,DestinationPrefix,NextHop,Metric –autosize

PSComputerName VirtualSubnetID DestinationPrefix NextHop Metric
-------------- --------------- ----------------- ------- ------
HVHost1   10   192.168.1.0/24   0.0.0.0 0
HVHost1   11   172.16.0.0/24   0.0.0.0 0

PS C:\> get-NetVirtualizationCustomerRoute -cimsession "HVHost2"| sort VirtualSubnetId,PSComputerName,DestinationPrefix | ft PSComputerName,VirtualSubnetID,DestinationPrefix,NextHop,Metric –autosize

PSComputerName VirtualSubnetID DestinationPrefix NextHop Metric
-------------- --------------- ----------------- ------- ------
HVHost1   10   192.168.1.0/24   0.0.0.0 0
HVHost1   11   172.16.0.0/24   0.0.0.0 0

In this output, look for the following:

- Whether each host has a record with a destination prefix for each virtual machine subnet
- Whether a record exists with a destination prefix of 0.0.0.0/0 (in which case the NextHop information identifies the WNV gateway)

Step 5: Check that each virtual machine's host has the same provider address that was specified in the lookup records

The provider address is the address used by a host for all Network Virtualization traffic from that host. With SCVMM managing the Network Virtualization environment, a unique provider address is needed for each virtual network on each host.

PS C:\> get-NetVirtualizationProviderAddress -CIMSession "HVHost1" | ft PSComputerName,ProviderAddress,PrefixLength,InterfaceIndex,VlanID -autosize

PSComputerName ProviderAddress PrefixLength InterfaceIndex VlanID
-------------- --------------- ------------ -------------- ------
HVHOST1   10.0.0.100   24   12   0

```
HVHOST1      10.0.0.101          24         12    0
```

```
PS C:\> get-NetVirtualizationProviderAddress -CIMSession "HVHost2" | ft
PSComputerName,ProviderAddress,PrefixLength,InterfaceIndex,VlanID -autosize

PSComputerName ProviderAddress PrefixLength InterfaceIndex VlanID
-------------- --------------- ------------ -------------- ------
HVHOST2        10.0.1.200       24           11             0
HVHOST2        10.0.1.200       24           11             0
```

In this output, verify that the provider addresses on each host match the addresses in the lookup records (from step 2). These addresses are assigned by SCVMM using the IP pool associated with the logical network connected to the host's network adapter(s).

Step 6: Check that the provider routes are correct on each host

These provider routes should contain the information needed to route between provider addresses in different subnets.

```
PS C:\> get-NetVirtualizationProviderRoute -CIMSession "HVHost1" | ft
PSComputerName,DestinationPrefix,NextHop,InterfaceIndex,Metric -autosize

PSComputerName DestinationPrefix NextHop  InterfaceIndex Metric
-------------- ----------------- -------  -------------- ------
HVHOST1        0.0.0.0/0         10.0.1.1       12        0
```

```
PS C:\> get-NetVirtualizationProviderRoute -CIMSession "HVHost2" | ft
PSComputerName,DestinationPrefix,NextHop,InterfaceIndex,Metric -autosize

PSComputerName DestinationPrefix NextHop  InterfaceIndex Metric
-------------- ----------------- -------  -------------- ------
HVHOST2        0.0.0.0/0         10.0.0.1       11        0
```

In this output, look for the following:

- If the provider addresses are in different subnets, the route information specified the NextHop or gateway to send traffic to the subnet of each remote provider address. Depending on the configuration used, the DestinationPrefix may be a specific subnet or 0.0.0.0/0 (which indicates the default route).

- The priority of routes (if more than one is available) as identified by the Metric setting.

- The network interface the route corresponds to as shown by the interface index (matches that displayed in the output from get-NetVirtualizationProviderAddress in the previous step).

Step 7: Check that each host has Network Virtualization bound to a network adapter

The host will use the identified network adapter for all Network Virtualization traffic. This is typically a teamed network adapter. This should not be a virtual adapter connected to the virtual switch. It can be the same adapter that a virtual switch is bound to. This should be the same adapter as listed in the provider routes.

PS C:\> get-netadapterbinding -CIMSession HVHOST1 | where {$_.ComponentID -eq "ms_netwnv" -and $_.enabled} | ft name,interfacedescription,componentid -autosize

```
name     interfacedescription                              componentid
----     --------------------                              -----------
Ethernet Broadcom NetXtreme 57xx Gigabit Controller        ms_netwnv
```

PS C:\> get-netadapterbinding -CIMSession HVHOST2 | where {$_.ComponentID -eq "ms_netwnv" -and $_.enabled} | ft name,interfacedescription,componentid -autosize

```
name     interfacedescription                              componentid
----     --------------------                              -----------
NICTeam  Microsoft Network Adapter Multiplexor Driver      ms_netwnv
```

In this output, look for the following:

- Whether each host has an adapter bound to the Network Virtualization driver (ms_netwnv). Even if no communication is occurring through Network Virtualization to a different host, for Network Virtualization to work, one adapter must be bound to the driver.
- Whether the name and description match the expected network adapter on the host. In the second example above, it is bound to a Microsoft Teaming adapter.

This is also indicated in the network adapter properties when the Windows Network Virtualization Filter driver option is selected—as shown here:

Putting it all together

Here are the same commands in one larger PowerShell script, with some additional formatting and a little more information being displayed.

This script contains two variables that need to be set ($HostNames and $VMNames). It can be run from any Windows 8 or Windows Server 2012 machine that has the Hyper-V Management features enabled and network connectivity to the machines defined in $HostNames. Only an administrator account on the Hyper-V machines can run the script:

```
# This example script will collect & display the information for Network Virtualization routing between two virtual machines on different hosts

# Set the variables $hostname and $VMNames before running this script.
# Hostnames is the computer name of each host
$HostNames = "Host1","Host2"

# VMNames is the name of each VM as it appears in the VMM console or
# Hyper-V Manager console
$VMNames = "VM1"," VM2"

write-host "1. Check each VM has the same VirtualSubnetId
" -ForegroundColor Cyan
$HostNames | %{get-vmnetworkadapter -all -computername $_} |
   where {$VMNames -contains $_.VMName} |
   ft computername,vmname,macaddress,virtualsubnetid,ipaddresses,status –autosize

write-host "2. Check that the lookup records are correct on each host for the VMs.
  Check:
    a. the virtualization lookup record for each VM is identical on all hosts,
    b. the customer address matches the VM's IP address settings
    c. the record information for the host name, MACAddress and
       VirtualSubnetID match what was displayed for each VM in step 1.
  The ProviderAddress value is used in later steps
" -ForegroundColor Cyan
$r = $HostNames | %{Get-NetVirtualizationLookupRecord -CIMSession $_} |
  where {$VMNames -contains $_.VMName}
$r | sort VMName,PSComputername |
  group VMname,MACAddress |
  %{$_.group | ft PScomputername,VMName,MacAddress,VirtualSubnetID,CustomerAddress,ProviderAddress -AutoSize}

#collect provider addresses - used later
$ProviderAddresses = $r | %{$_.provideraddress} | select -unique
#collect the VirtualSubnetIDs - used later
$VirtualSubnetIDs = $r | %{$_.VirtualSubnetID} | select -unique
#Identify the WNV gateway addresses - used later
```

```
$CA_SubnetGW = $r | %{$_.CustomerAddress} |
    %{$_.substring(0,$_.LastIndexOf("."))+".1"} | select -unique
```

write-host "3. Check that a WNV subnet gateway address exists on each host for the virtual machines.
   Check:
      a. each host has a record with a '.1' address in each subnet
         This is an reserved address for the purpose of routing between
         subnets within a VM network
      b. if any records identify a virtual machine, the default routing between
         subnets will no longer work
" -ForegroundColor Cyan

```
$HostNames | %{Get-NetVirtualizationLookupRecord -CIMSession $_} |
   where {$CA_SubnetGW -contains $_.CustomerAddress -and
        $VirtualSubnetIDs -contains $_.VirtualSubnetID} |
   sort VMName,PSComputername | group VMName |
   %{$_.group | ft PScomputername,VMName,MacAddress,VirtualSubnetID,CustomerAddress,ProviderAddress -AutoSize}
```

write-host "4. Check that a WNV route exists on each host for each subnet in the VM network.
   Check:
      a. each host has a record with a destination prefix for each VMs subnet
      b. if a record exists with a destination prefix of 0.0.0.0/0, then
         the nexthop information identifies the WNV Gateway
" -ForegroundColor Cyan

```
$HostNames | %{get-NetVirtualizationCustomerRoute -CIMSession $_} |
   where {$VirtualSubnetIDs -contains $_.VirtualSubnetID} |
   sort VirtualSubnetId,PSComputerName,DestinationPrefix |
   ft PSComputerName,VirtualSubnetID,DestinationPrefix,NextHop,Metric -autosize
```

write-host "5. Check that each virtual machine's host has the same provider
   address that was specified in the lookup records.
   SCVMM will assign a provider address for each virtual subnet on each host
" -ForegroundColor Cyan

```
$HostNames | %{get-NetVirtualizationProviderAddress -CIMSession $_} |
   where {$provideraddresses -contains $_.providerAddress} |
   ft PSComputerName,ProviderAddress,PrefixLength,InterfaceIndex,VlanID -autosize
```

write-host "6. Check the provider routes are correct on each host
   (this may be blank if the provider addresses are in the same subnet)
" -ForegroundColor Cyan

```
$HostNames | %{get-NetVirtualizationProviderRoute -CIMSession $_} |
   ft PSComputerName,DestinationPrefix,NextHop,InterfaceIndex,Metric -autosize
```

write-host "7. Check that each host has Network Virtualization bound to a
   network adapter. If a host is not listed, this indicates that no network

adapters have Network Virtualization bound to them.

The ifIndex should match the interface index values in the provider

addresses and provider routes above

" -ForegroundColor Cyan

$HostNames | %{get-netadapterbinding -CIMSession $_} |

where {$_.ComponentID -eq "ms_netwnv" -and $_.enabled} |

get-netadapter |

ft PSComputerName,ifindex,name,status,linkspeed,interfacedescription -autosize

> **TIP** You can download a zip file containing this Windows PowerShell script from http://aka.ms/TroubleshootHyper-VNetworking/files.

—Nick Eales, Senior Premier Field Engineer

Tracing the VMM Network Virtualization components

In System Center 2012 VMM SP1, the VMM server is responsible for automatically updating each VMM host with updated lookup and customer route records as needed. Each VMM host will be provisioned with a subset of the entire address virtualization mapping table as needed based on the network configuration in use by the virtual machines hosted on each server.

> **NOTE** If you find a discrepancy in the lookup records published to a VMM-managed host, you must resolve the configuration issue within VMM. If you manually add a Provider Address, Customer Address, or Customer Route using the Set-NetVirtualization Windows PowerShell cmdlets, the manually added settings will be overwritten by VMM during the next polling cycle (every 10 minutes).

When troubleshooting communication issues between virtual machines using Network Virtualization, a network capture taken on the virtual machines themselves will typically not be useful. Since the routing between Customer Address space and Provider Address space is done within the software running on the VMM host, packets may simply disappear from the standpoint of Network Monitor captures. To see the reason for packet drops in the WNV extension, you must enable logging specific to the WNV provider. This logging must be enabled on the VMM host server.

First, use the output of Get-NetVirtualizationLookupRecord and Get-NetVirtualizationCustomerRoute Windows PowerShell cmdlets to identify the VSID (VirtualSubnetID) and RDID (CustomerID) that is associated with each Customer Address assigned to the virtual machines. These same RDID and VSID values must exist on the target VMM host in order for routing to function within the Network Virtualization environment.

Then, trace the WNV provider using the netsh trace context on both sender and target VMM host servers. Examine the trace file to determine whether incoming packets were successfully matched to a corresponding Network Virtualization lookup record.

Use Windows PowerShell to display configuration

You can use the following two NetWNV Windows PowerShell Cmdlets to display the current lookup policies assigned to a VMM host:

- Get-NetVirtualizationLookupRecord
- Get-NetVirtualizationCustomerRoute

NOTE For more information about WNV Windows PowerShell cmdlet syntax and usage, see "NetWNV Cmdlets in Windows PowerShell" at http://technet.microsoft.com/en-us/library/jj884262.aspx.

Get-NetVirtualizationLookupRecord

The syntax for the Get-NetVirtualizationLookupRecord cmdlet is as follows:

Get-NetVirtualizationLookupRecord [-AsJob] [-CimSession <CimSession[]>] [-Context <String[]>] [-CustomerAddress <String[]>] [-CustomerID <String[]>] [-MACAddress <String[]>] [-ProviderAddress <String[]>] [-Rule <RuleType[]>] [-ThrottleLimit <Int32>] [-UseVmMACAddress <Boolean[]>] [-VirtualSubnetID <UInt32[]>] [-VMName <String[]>] [<CommonParameters>]

Here is some sample output from running this cmdlet:

CustomerAddress : 10.254.254.2
VirtualSubnetID : 12243999
MACAddress   : 00cafedec0c1
ProviderAddress : 192.168.0.200
CustomerID   : {769B93BD-967D-439D-B197-298DA4C3BFC0}
Context   : SCVMM-MANAGED
Rule   : TranslationMethodEncap
VMName   : GW-External
UseVmMACAddress : False

CustomerAddress : 10.0.1.100
VirtualSubnetID : 3211815
MACAddress   : 001dd8b71c00
ProviderAddress : 192.168.0.100
CustomerID   : {25AE978C-AAD1-4F13-B913-B310F4C52129}
Context   : SCVMM-MANAGED
Rule   : TranslationMethodEncap
VMName   : Contoso APP1
UseVmMACAddress : False

CustomerAddress : 10.254.254.2
VirtualSubnetID : 1579966
MACAddress   : 00cafedec0c0
ProviderAddress : 192.168.0.200
CustomerID   : {25AE978C-AAD1-4F13-B913-B310F4C52129}
Context   : SCVMM-MANAGED
Rule   : TranslationMethodEncap
VMName   : GW-External
UseVmMACAddress : False

CustomerAddress : 10.0.1.1
VirtualSubnetID : 4746905
MACAddress   : 005056000001
ProviderAddress : 1.1.1.1
CustomerID   : {769B93BD-967D-439D-B197-298DA4C3BFC0}
Context   : SCVMM-MANAGED
Rule   : TranslationMethodEncap
VMName   : GW
UseVmMACAddress : False

CustomerAddress : 10.0.1.1
VirtualSubnetID : 3211815
MACAddress   : 005056000000
ProviderAddress : 1.1.1.1
CustomerID   : {25AE978C-AAD1-4F13-B913-B310F4C52129}
Context   : SCVMM-MANAGED
Rule   : TranslationMethodEncap
VMName   : GW
UseVmMACAddress : False

CustomerAddress : 10.0.1.100
VirtualSubnetID : 4746905
MACAddress   : 001dd8b71c01
ProviderAddress : 192.168.0.101
CustomerID   : {769B93BD-967D-439D-B197-298DA4C3BFC0}
Context   : SCVMM-MANAGED
Rule   : TranslationMethodEncap
VMName   : Fabrikam APP1
UseVmMACAddress : False

Get-NetVirtualizationCustomerRoute

The syntax for the Get-NetVirtualizationCustomerRoute cmdlet is as follows:

Get-NetVirtualizationCustomerRoute [-AsJob] [-CimSession <CimSession[]>] [-DestinationPrefix <String[]>] [-Metric

`<UInt32[]>`] [-NextHop `<String[]>`] [-RoutingDomainID `<String[]>`] [-ThrottleLimit `<Int32>`] [-VirtualSubnetID `<UInt32[]>`]
[`<CommonParameters>`]

Here is some sample output from running this cmdlet:

RoutingDomainID : {769B93BD-967D-439D-B197-298DA4C3BFC0}
VirtualSubnetID : 4746905
DestinationPrefix : 10.0.1.0/24
NextHop   : 0.0.0.0
Metric   : 0

RoutingDomainID : {769B93BD-967D-439D-B197-298DA4C3BFC0}
VirtualSubnetID : 12243999
DestinationPrefix : 0.0.0.0/0
NextHop   : 10.254.254.2
Metric   : 0

RoutingDomainID : {25AE978C-AAD1-4F13-B913-B310F4C52129}
VirtualSubnetID : 3211815
DestinationPrefix : 10.0.1.0/24
NextHop   : 0.0.0.0
Metric   : 0

RoutingDomainID : {25AE978C-AAD1-4F13-B913-B310F4C52129}
VirtualSubnetID : 1579966
DestinationPrefix : 0.0.0.0/0
NextHop   : 10.254.254.2
Metric   : 0

Tracing VmSwitch and WNV

Use the following steps to enable tracing for WNV and the Hyper-V VmSwitch:

1. Run the following cmdlet:

    netsh trace start provider=Microsoft-Windows-WNV provider=Microsoft-Windows-Hyper-V-VmSwitch tracefile=C:\NetTrace.etl

2. Reproduce the connectivity failure or issue being investigated.

3. Stop the trace with this command:

    netsh trace stop

4. Convert the trace to a text file with this command:

    netsh trace convert C:\NetTrace.etl C:\NetTraceOutput.txt

Following packets routed through WNV

Examine the NetTraceOutput.txt file to see successful routing of packets that match the lookup policies (please note the bolded output):

0229 [2]0000.0000::2013-01-16 11:58:24.427 [Microsoft-Windows-Hyper-V-VmSwitch]NBL routed from Nic /DEVICE/{37242363-3C54-452E-B231-58C454535C5D} (Friendly Name: Broadcom BCM5709C NetXtreme II GigE (NDIS VBD Client) #32) to Nic D165E799-3016-4FE1-9679-431E55DE5B35 (Friendly Name: Hosternet) on switch 05C5AF25-7C82-4405-AAAD-D002533F38D2 (Friendly Name: Hosternet)

0230 [2]0000.0000::2013-01-16 11:58:24.427 [Microsoft-Windows-Hyper-V-VmSwitch]NBL delivered to Nic D165E799-3016-4FE1-9679-431E55DE5B35 (Friendly Name: Hosternet) in switch 05C5AF25-7C82-4405-AAAD-D002533F38D2 (Friendly Name: Hosternet)

0232 [0]0000.0000::2013-01-16 11:58:24.524 [Microsoft-Windows-Hyper-V-VmSwitch]NBL **received from Nic** D5DDF06B-52BB-4D42-89FC-EA7B89CB014C--7671D51F-F8C0-4538-B567-BBF40DA6034A (Friendly Name: Contoso APP1) in switch 05C5AF25-7C82-4405-AAAD-D002533F38D2 (Friendly Name: Hosternet)

0233 [0]0000.0000::2013-01-16 11:58:24.524 [Microsoft-Windows-Hyper-V-VmSwitch]NBL **routed from Nic** D5DDF06B-52BB-4D42-89FC-EA7B89CB014C--7671D51F-F8C0-4538-B567-BBF40DA6034A (Friendly Name: Contoso APP1) to Nic /DEVICE/{37242363-3C54-452E-B231-58C454535C5D} (Friendly Name: Broadcom BCM5709C NetXtreme II GigE (NDIS VBD Client) #32) on switch 05C5AF25-7C82-4405-AAAD-D002533F38D2 (Friendly Name: Hosternet)

0234 [0]0000.0000::2013-01-16 11:58:24.524 [Microsoft-Windows-Hyper-V-VmSwitch]NBL **delivered to Nic** /DEVICE/{37242363-3C54-452E-B231-58C454535C5D} (Friendly Name: Broadcom BCM5709C NetXtreme II GigE (NDIS VBD Client) #32) in switch 05C5AF25-7C82-4405-AAAD-D002533F38D2 (Friendly Name: Hosternet)

0235 [0]0000.0000::2013-01-16 11:58:24.524 [Microsoft-Windows-Wnv]**Outbound packet processing lookup succeeded:** Source IP in packet: 10.0.1.100, Destination IP in packet: 10.0.0.1, Source IP in record: 192.168.0.100, Destination IP in record: 192.168.0.200, VirtualNexthopIpAddress: 10.254.254.2, ProviderNexthopIpAddress: , SourceCAMac: 0x001DD8B71C00, DestinationCAMac: 0x005056000000, Source MAC in record: 0x001DD8B71C00, Destination MAC in record: 0x00CAFEDEC0C0, Outer source IP: , Outer destination IP:

0236 [1]0000.0000::2013-01-16 11:58:24.525 [Microsoft-Windows-Wnv]**Inbound packet processing lookup succeeded:** Source IP in packet: 10.0.0.1, Destination IP in packet: 10.0.1.100, Source IP in record: 192.168.0.200, Destination IP in record: 192.168.0.100, VirtualNexthopIpAddress: 10.254.254.2, ProviderNexthopIpAddress: , SourceCAMac: 0x00CAFEDEC0C0, DestinationCAMac: 0x001DD8B71C00, Source MAC in record: 0x00CAFEDEC0C0, Destination MAC in record: 0x001DD8B71C00, Outer source IP: 192.168.0.200, Outer destination IP: 192.168.0.100

Troubleshooting dropped packets

If a packet is dropped by the WNV provider, trace events should be logged to indicate the reason, such as failure to find a matching policy, VSID, or source locator record (please note the bolded output):

0226 [2]0000.0000::2013-01-16 11:58:24.427 [Microsoft-Windows-Hyper-V-VmSwitch]NBL destined to Nic 9F43D7EB-B152-46D7-B628-DD0240B2F63B--AA00D6B0-64F0-4EAD-8C87-2844FD4DFEBE (Friendly Name: Fabrikam APP1) was dropped in switch 05C5AF25-7C82-4405-AAAD-D002533F38D2 (Friendly Name: Hosternet), **Reason Virtual Subnet ID does not match**

0228 [2]0000.0000::2013-01-16 11:58:24.427 [Microsoft-Windows-Hyper-V-VmSwitch]NBL destined to Nic D5DDF06B-52BB-4D42-89FC-EA7B89CB014C--7671D51F-F8C0-4538-B567-BBF40DA6034A (Friendly Name: Contoso APP1) was dropped in switch 05C5AF25-7C82-4405-AAAD-D002533F38D2 (Friendly Name: Hosternet), **Reason Virtual Subnet ID does not match**

001 [0]0000.0000::2013-01-09 13:02:40.336 [Microsoft-Windows-Wnv]Inbound packet processing lookup failure: Source IP in packet: 10.0.1.100, Destination IP in packet: 10.0.0.1, Source IP in record: , Destination IP in record: , VirtualNexthopIpAddress: , ProviderNexthopIpAddress: , **Failure Reason: Source locator record missing**, SourceCAMac: 0x001DD8B71C12, DestinationCAMac: 0x00CAFEDEC0C1, Source MAC in record: 0x000000000000, Destination MAC in record: 0x000000000000, Outer source IP: 192.168.0.101, Outer destination IP: 192.168.0.200

002 [0]0000.0000::2013-01-09 13:02:42.248 [Microsoft-Windows-Wnv]Inbound packet processing lookup failure: Source IP in packet: 10.0.1.100, Destination IP in packet: 10.0.0.1, Source IP in record: , Destination IP in record: , VirtualNexthopIpAddress: , ProviderNexthopIpAddress: , **Failure Reason: Source locator record missing**, SourceCAMac: 0x001DD8B71C12, DestinationCAMac: 0x00CAFEDEC0C1, Source MAC in record: 0x000000000000, Destination MAC in record: 0x000000000000, Outer source IP: 192.168.0.101, Outer destination IP: 192.168.0.200

Enable debug logging in System Center 2012 VMM SP1

NOTE For details about how to enable debug logging for System Center 2012 VMM SP1, see KB article 2801185 at http://support.microsoft.com/kb/2801185.

To enable VMM debug logging, use the following steps:

1. Create a folder called C:\vmmlogs.
2. Open an elevated Windows PowerShell window on the VMM server or host computer and run the following commands (the second command may wrap in your display):

    logman delete VMM

    (This deletes any existing definitions of the trace. "Data Collector Set was not found" errors can be safely ignored.)

    logman create trace VMM -v mmddhhmm -o $env:SystemDrive\VMMlogs\VMMLog_$env:computername.ETL -cnf 01:00:00 -p Microsoft-VirtualMachineManager-Debug -nb 10 250 -bs 16 -max 512 -a

3. Start the trace by typing the following command in the elevated PowerShell window:

    logman start VMM

4. Reproduce your issue.
5. As soon as you reproduce your issue, stop the trace by typing:

    logman stop VMM

    The ETL file can be found in C:\VMMlogs.

6. To convert the trace, type the command:

    Netsh trace convert <filename>

    where *<filename>* is the name of the ETL file from step 5. The converted trace file will be named in the format <filename>.txt.

VMM DHCP Server tracing

The debug logging described above does not capture tracing of the System Center Virtual Machine Manager DHCP Server. This component is installed automatically as part of the provisioning process when a Hyper-V host is added under VMM management. The Microsoft VMM DHCP Server Switch Extension is bound to the Hyper-V standard switch or VMM logical switch on which Network Virtualization is enabled. This DHCP switch extension is the component responsible for providing CA addresses to virtual machines from the IP pool associated with the virtual machine network in VMM.

If you need to troubleshoot assignment of addresses to virtual machines, trace the VMM DHCP provider using the following steps.

1. Start the trace by typing the following command in an elevated Windows PowerShell window:

   Netsh trace start provider=Microsoft-VirtualMachineManager-DHCPServer tracefile=C:\VMMLogs\VMMDHCP.etl

2. Reproduce your issue, or attempt to obtain a DHCP address on a guest virtual machine.

3. As soon as you reproduce your issue, stop the trace by typing:

   Netsh trace stop

4. To convert the trace, type the command:

   Netsh trace convert C:\VMMLogs\VMMDHCP.etl

   The converted trace file will be named VMMDHCP.txt.

Here is some sample DHCP trace output showing a successful address release and renewal (please note the bolded output):

[1]0004.0324::2013-02-13 11:54:57.628 [Microsoft-VirtualMachineManager-DHCPServer]Processing DHCPv4 message with Transaction ID 0x303036B1 for switch port 4.

[1]0004.0324::2013-02-13 11:54:57.628 [Microsoft-VirtualMachineManager-DHCPServer]The DHCPv4 server on (Switch, PortId, PortName) = (Hosternet, 4, D53BEEFC-F082-4C78-A393-6F51F91F1A5B) has received a message from a client. The type of the message is **Release** . The DHCP message flags are 0x0. The source IP/MAC are 10.0.1.100/0x001DD8B71C01. The destination IP/MAC are 10.0.0.1/0x005056000003. The Client Hardware Address is 0x001DD8B71C0100000000000000000000, The yiaddr value is 0.0.0.0, the ciaddr value is 10.0.1.100, the siaddr value is 0.0.0.0 and the giaddr value is 0.0.0.0.

[1]0004.0324::2013-02-13 11:54:57.628 [Microsoft-VirtualMachineManager-DHCPServer]The DHCPv4 server on (Switch, PortId, PortName) = (Hosternet, 4, D53BEEFC-F082-4C78-A393-6F51F91F1A5B) received a RELEASE message. The destination IPv4 was 10.0.0.1 and the destination MAC was 0x005056000003. **The binding is released.**
[1]0004.12A4::2013-02-13 11:55:03.926 [Microsoft-VirtualMachineManager-DHCPServer]Processing DHCPv4 message with Transaction ID 0xD6A30DFD for switch port 4.

[1]0004.12A4::2013-02-13 11:55:03.926 [Microsoft-VirtualMachineManager-DHCPServer]The DHCPv4 server on (Switch, PortId, PortName) = (Hosternet, 4, D53BEEFC-F082-4C78-A393-6F51F91F1A5B) has received a message from a client. The type of the message is **Discover** . The DHCP message flags are 0x0. The source IP/MAC are 0.0.0.0/0x001DD8B71C01. The destination IP/MAC are 255.255.255.255/0xFFFFFFFFFFFF. The Client Hardware Address is 0x001DD8B71C010000000000000000000000, The yiaddr value is 0.0.0.0, the ciaddr value is 0.0.0.0, the siaddr value is 0.0.0.0 and the giaddr value is 0.0.0.0.

[1]0004.12A4::2013-02-13 11:55:03.926 [Microsoft-VirtualMachineManager-DHCPServer]The DHCPv4 server on (Switch, PortId, PortName) = (Hosternet, 4, D53BEEFC-F082-4C78-A393-6F51F91F1A5B) is sending a message to a client. Some fields in this message may be overwritten during address resolution. The type of the message is **Offer** . The DHCP message flags are 0x0. The source IP/MAC are 10.0.0.1/0x1234567890AB. The destination IP/MAC are 10.0.1.100/0x001DD8B71C01. The Client Hardware Address is 0x001DD8B71C010000000000000000000000, The yiaddr value is 10.0.1.100, the ciaddr value is 0.0.0.0, the siaddr value is 10.0.0.1 and the giaddr value is 10.0.1.1.

[1]0004.12A4::2013-02-13 11:55:03.926 [Microsoft-VirtualMachineManager-DHCPServer]The next hop IPv4 address and source MAC address have been resolved as 10.0.1.100 and 0x1234567890AB, respectively, based upon the source IPv4 address of 10.0.0.1 and the destination IPv4 address of 10.0.1.100.
[1]0004.12A4::2013-02-13 11:55:03.926 [Microsoft-VirtualMachineManager-DHCPServer]The extension-based client on the switch named {Hosternet} has sent a network packet identified as 0xFFFFFA8014586030 from pool 0xFFFFFA8007EDE040.

[1]0004.12A4::2013-02-13 11:55:03.926 [Microsoft-VirtualMachineManager-DHCPServer]The extension-based client on the switch named {Hosternet} has completed a network packet identified as 0xFFFFFA8014586030 from pool 0xFFFFFA8007EDE040 with status STATUS_SUCCESS.
[1]0004.12A4::2013-02-13 11:55:03.926 [Microsoft-VirtualMachineManager-DHCPServer]Processing DHCPv4 message with Transaction ID 0xD6A30DFD for switch port 4.

[1]0004.12A4::2013-02-13 11:55:03.926 [Microsoft-VirtualMachineManager-DHCPServer]The DHCPv4 server on (Switch, PortId, PortName) = (Hosternet, 4, D53BEEFC-F082-4C78-A393-6F51F91F1A5B) has received a message from a client. The type of the message is **Request**. The DHCP message flags are 0x0. The source IP/MAC are 0.0.0.0/0x001DD8B71C01. The destination IP/MAC are 255.255.255.255/0xFFFFFFFFFFFF. The Client Hardware Address is 0x001DD8B71C0100000000000000000000, The yiaddr value is 0.0.0.0, the ciaddr value is 0.0.0.0, the siaddr value is 0.0.0.0 and the giaddr value is 0.0.0.0.

[1]0004.12A4::2013-02-13 11:55:03.926 [Microsoft-VirtualMachineManager-DHCPServer]The DHCPv4 server on (Switch, PortId, PortName) = (Hosternet, 4, D53BEEFC-F082-4C78-A393-6F51F91F1A5B) is sending a message to a client. Some fields in this message may be overwritten during address resolution. The type of the message is **Ack**. The DHCP message flags are 0x0. The source IP/MAC are 10.0.0.1/0x1234567890AB. The destination IP/MAC are 10.0.1.100/0x001DD8B71C01. The Client Hardware Address is 0x001DD8B71C0100000000000000000000, The yiaddr value is 10.0.1.100, the ciaddr value is 0.0.0.0, the siaddr value is 0.0.0.0 and the giaddr value is 10.0.1.1.

[1]0004.12A4::2013-02-13 11:55:03.926 [Microsoft-VirtualMachineManager-DHCPServer]The next hop IPv4 address and source MAC address have been resolved as 10.0.1.100 and 0x1234567890AB, respectively, based upon the source IPv4 address of 10.0.0.1 and the destination IPv4 address of 10.0.1.100.

[1]0004.12A4::2013-02-13 11:55:03.926 [Microsoft-VirtualMachineManager-DHCPServer]The extension-based client on the switch named {Hosternet} has sent a network packet identified as 0xFFFFFA8014586030 from pool 0xFFFFFA8007EDE040.

[1]0004.12A4::2013-02-13 11:55:03.926 [Microsoft-VirtualMachineManager-DHCPServer]The extension-based client on the switch named {Hosternet} has completed a network packet identified as 0xFFFFFA8014586030 from pool 0xFFFFFA8007EDE040 with status STATUS_SUCCESS.

—Tim Quinn, Support Escalation Engineer, Windows Platform Distributed Systems Networking

Additional resources

Here is an additional resource concerning this topic:

- Hyper-V Network Virtualization Overview (TechNet Library) at: http://technet.microsoft.com/en-us/library/jj134230.aspx

Automating network settings for hosts

Sometimes the best way to troubleshoot something is to avoid problems in the first place. Complex Hyper-V configurations can be time consuming to set up manually and can lead to issues that are hard to troubleshoot. Windows PowerShell is so useful because you can use it to automate the configuration process to ensure it's free of errors. Of course that means your Windows PowerShell commands and scripts must also be free of errors.

A good way to learn how to create error-free configuration scripts is to study and then customize scripts created by experts. In this section, Trevor Cooper-Chadwick, a Principle Consultant with Microsoft Consulting Services UK, demonstrates how to use Windows PowerShell to automate the setup of a large number of Hyper-V hosts.

Automating the setup of a large number of Hyper-V hosts

Have you ever been faced with building out a Hyper-V cluster across multiple HP blades using non-converged networking and FlexNICs? System Center 2012 Virtual Machine Manager (VMM) does a great job through its bare metal provisioning to get the host operating system deployed, but often you are then faced with creating multiple LBFO (Load Balancing and Fail Over) teams across the hosts and several virtual switches. Performing this manually is a somewhat tedious and error-prone task because device names are rarely consistent across the hosts and so each and every adapter has to be identified by MAC address and assigned accordingly. No fun when you're dealing with 160 adapters!

My scenario was a fairly typical non-converged infrastructure pattern with the host networks (Management, Live Migration, and Cluster) separated in the physical switch layer from the virtual machine trunked networks (and I had two of these in this case). For resilience, each of these five networks required dual redundant paths, so that's 10 adapters per host to identify and place into the correct LBFO teams.

The diagram on the following page shows the configuration of adapters, teams, and virtual switches I was looking to configure on each of the blades.

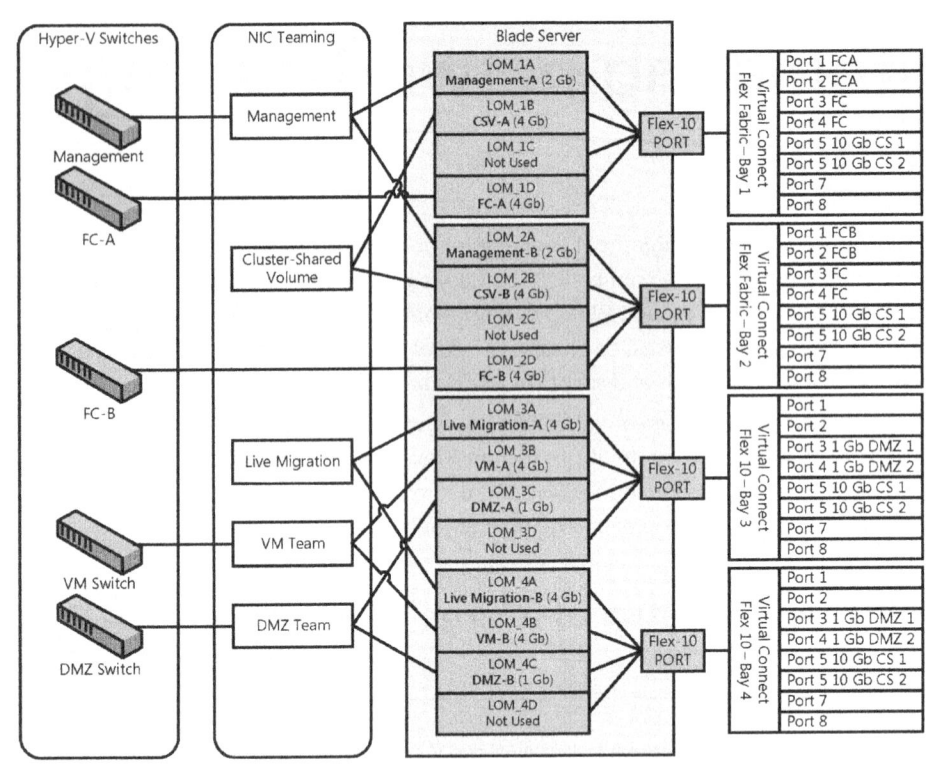

Hyper-V Switches	NIC Teaming	Blade Server		Virtual Connect Flex Fabric – Bay 1
Management	Management	LOM_1A Management-A (2 Gb)	Flex-10 PORT	Port 1 FCA / Port 2 FCA / Port 3 FC / Port 4 FC / Port 5 10 Gb CS 1 / Port 5 10 Gb CS 2 / Port 7 / Port 8
		LOM_1B CSV-A (4 Gb)		
		LOM_1C Not Used		
FC-A	Cluster-Shared Volume	LOM_1D FC-A (4 Gb)		
		LOM_2A Management-B (2 Gb)	Flex-10 PORT	Port 1 FCB / Port 2 FCB / Port 3 FC / Port 4 FC / Port 5 10 Gb CS 1 / Port 5 10 Gb CS 2 / Port 7 / Port 8 (Virtual Connect Flex Fabric – Bay 2)
		LOM_2B CSV-B (4 Gb)		
		LOM_2C Not Used		
FC-B	Live Migration	LOM_2D FC-B (4 Gb)		
		LOM_3A Live Migration-A (4 Gb)	Flex-10 PORT	Port 1 / Port 2 / Port 3 1 Gb DMZ 1 / Port 4 1 Gb DMZ 2 / Port 5 10 Gb CS 1 / Port 5 10 Gb CS 2 / Port 7 / Port 8 (Virtual Connect Flex 10 – Bay 3)
		LOM_3B VM-A (4 Gb)		
	VM Team	LOM_3C DMZ-A (1 Gb)		
VM Switch		LOM_3D Not Used		
	DMZ Team	LOM_4A Live Migration-B (4 Gb)	Flex-10 PORT	Port 1 / Port 2 / Port 3 1 Gb DMZ 1 / Port 4 1 Gb DMZ 2 / Port 5 10 Gb CS 1 / Port 5 10 Gb CS 2 / Port 7 / Port 8 (Virtual Connect Flex 10 – Bay 4)
DMZ Switch		LOM_4B VM-B (4 Gb)		
		LOM_4C DMZ-B (1 Gb)		
		LOM_4D Not Used		

Of course while this looks great in the design document, when I came to the task of creating the teams, although the LOM (LAN-on-Motherboard) configuration is consistent across the hosts, the NIC enumeration was most definitely not. So although, for example, the Management LBFO Team might require pairing the Broadcom BCM5708S NetXtreme II GigE (NDIS VBD Client) #34 with the Broadcom BCM5708S NetXtreme II GigE (NDIS VBD Client) #38 on one host, this was not the case for any other host in the cluster. In order to identify the correct pairs of adapters to team, each and every adapter would have to be examined to find its MAC address (allocated by HP Flex Connect) to determine the LOM and which team it belonged to. A tedious task and very error prone. To make matters worse, any errors could lead to a range of intermittent or seemingly random network issues—poor network performance, virtual machines losing connectivity, cluster networking errors—all of which can be very challenging and time consuming to track down.

Wouldn't it be great if we could just automate this?

Well, we can. PowerShell has commands to create LBFO Teams and virtual switches. However, to automate this task fully, we must start with consistently identifying the adapters across all the hosts. The key to this is to re-label the adapters using the MAC addresses taken from the HP Flex Fabric with common names across the hosts.

For each host (or Device Bay in HP Flex Connect parlance) we can obtain the MAC addresses from the HP Flex Connect console or, to make cut and paste a little easier, export the HP Flex Connect configuration into a text file. This may be done using the following steps:

1. Log in to the HP c7000 Onboard Administrator via a browser.
2. On the menu on the left, click Enclosure Setting.
3. Click Configuration Scripts.
4. Click Click Here To View A Script Containing A List Of The Enclosure Current Inventory.

This will save a .txt file with a dump of the entire HP c7000 configuration. If you search through the file and look for ">SHOW SERVER INFO ALL", there will be a series of entries for each Device Bay (host) that will list the MAC and WWNs.

Using this information we can populate our script with the host-specific information:

```
#Get the host name
$VMHOST = $env:COMPUTERNAME

#Relabel adapters
Switch ($VMHost)
{
  'HV0001' {
  $HyperV_Mgmt_A  = "00-17-A4-77-04-02"
  $CSV_A          = "00-17-A4-77-04-0A"
  $HyperV_Mgmt_B  = "00-17-A4-77-04-04"
  $CSV_B          = "00-17-A4-77-04-0C"
  $LiveMigration_A = "00-17-A4-77-04-06"
  $VM_A           = "00-17-A4-77-04-0E"
  $DMZ_A          = "00-17-A4-77-04-16"
  $LiveMigration_B = "00-17-A4-77-04-08"
  $VM_B           = "00-17-A4-77-04-10"
  $DMZ_B          = "00-17-A4-77-04-18"
  }
  'HV0002' {
  $HyperV_Mgmt_A  = "00-17-A4-77-04-20"
  $CSV_A          = "00-17-A4-77-04-28"
  $HyperV_Mgmt_B  = "00-17-A4-77-04-22"
  $CSV_B          = "00-17-A4-77-04-2A"
  $LiveMigration_A = "00-17-A4-77-04-24"
  $VM_A           = "00-17-A4-77-04-2C"
  $DMZ_A          = "00-17-A4-77-04-34"
  $LiveMigration_B = "00-17-A4-77-04-26"
  $VM_B           = "00-17-A4-77-04-2E"
  $DMZ_B          = "00-17-A4-77-04-36"
  }
  #....
```

}

Having set up the static data taken from HP Flex Connect, the following steps in the script are straightforward and common across all the hosts:

#Relabel adapters
Get-NetAdapter | where {$_.MacAddress -eq $HyperV_Mgmt_A } | Rename-NetAdapter -NewName HyperV-Mgmt-A
Get-NetAdapter | where {$_.MacAddress -eq $CSV_A   } | Rename-NetAdapter -NewName CSV-A
Get-NetAdapter | where {$_.MacAddress -eq $HyperV_Mgmt_B } | Rename-NetAdapter -NewName HyperV-Mgmt-B
Get-NetAdapter | where {$_.MacAddress -eq $CSV_B   } | Rename-NetAdapter -NewName CSV-B
Get-NetAdapter | where {$_.MacAddress -eq $LiveMigration_A} | Rename-NetAdapter -NewName LiveMigration-A
Get-NetAdapter | where {$_.MacAddress -eq $VM_A   } | Rename-NetAdapter -NewName VM-A
Get-NetAdapter | where {$_.MacAddress -eq $DMZ_A   } | Rename-NetAdapter -NewName DMZ-A
Get-NetAdapter | where {$_.MacAddress -eq $LiveMigration_B} | Rename-NetAdapter -NewName LiveMigration-B
Get-NetAdapter | where {$_.MacAddress -eq $VM_B   } | Rename-NetAdapter -NewName VM-B
Get-NetAdapter | where {$_.MacAddress -eq $DMZ_B   } | Rename-NetAdapter -NewName DMZ-B

This done, I still have some unused and unconfigured adapters on the host. To avoid these causing warnings later during cluster validation, I disable them:

#And disable anything we have not relabeled
Get-NetAdapter | where {("HyperV-Mgmt-A","HyperV-Mgmt-B","CSV-A","CSV-B","LiveMigration-A","LiveMigration-B","VM-A","VM-B","DMZ-A","DMZ-B" -notcontains $_.Name} | Disable-NetAdapter -Confirm:$false

With the adapters now consistently labeled, the LBFO teams are created:

#Create the teams
New-NetLbfoTeam -name "HyperV-Mgmt" -TeamMembers HyperV-Mgmt-A,HyperV-Mgmt-B -TeamingMode SwitchIndependent -LoadBalancingAlgorithm HyperVPort -Confirm:$false
New-NetLbfoTeam -name "ClusterSharedVolume" -TeamMembers CSV-A,CSV-B -TeamingMode SwitchIndependent -LoadBalancingAlgorithm HyperVPort -Confirm:$false
New-NetLbfoTeam -name "LiveMigration" -TeamMembers LiveMigration-A,LiveMigration-B -TeamingMode SwitchIndependent -LoadBalancingAlgorithm HyperVPort -Confirm:$false
New-NetLbfoTeam -name "VM Team" -TeamMembers VM-A,VM-B -TeamingMode SwitchIndependent -LoadBalancingAlgorithm HyperVPort -Confirm:$false
New-NetLbfoTeam -name "DMZ Team" -TeamMembers DMZ-A,DMZ-B -TeamingMode SwitchIndependent -LoadBalancingAlgorithm HyperVPort -Confirm:$false

VMM's bare metal provisioning deploys the host operating system and adds the Hyper-V role, but it does not add the Hyper-V PowerShell libraries. These will be needed to create the virtual switches:

#Add additional features
Add-WindowsFeature -Name Hyper-V-Powershell

Now the virtual switches can be created:

#Create Hyper-V Switches bound to team
New-VMSwitch -Name "HyperV-Mgmt" -AllowManagementOS $true -NetAdapterName "HyperV-Mgmt"
New-VMSwitch -Name "VM Switch" -AllowManagementOS $false -NetAdapterName "VM Team"
New-VMSwitch -Name "DMZ Switch" -AllowManagementOS $false -NetAdapterName "DMZ Team"

And that's it. Now a single script can be used to automate adapter relabeling, LBFO team creation, and virtual switch creation across all the hosts in a consistent and repeatable manner. It can be simply extended to assign IP addresses, since the team adapters now have consistent names, or it can be used to perform other tasks, such as creating virtual fibre channel switches.

I find it convenient to place this script into a custom resource (.CR) folder in the VMM Library and then use the VMM Run Script Command to execute it on each host after the initial bare metal provisioning has been completed.

This script made building out large numbers of (HP) Hyper-V hosts a lot less painful for me, and I hope it may also be of use to you.

TIP You can download a zip file containing this Windows PowerShell from http://aka.ms/TroubleshootHyper-VNetworking/files.

—*Trevor Cooper-Chadwick, Principle Consultant, Microsoft Consulting Services UK*

Additional resources

Here are a few additional resources concerning this topic:

- Windows PowerShell Support for Windows Server 2012 (TechNet Library) at:
  http://technet.microsoft.com/en-us/library/hh801904.aspx

- Windows Server 2012 NIC Teaming (LBFO) Deployment and Management (Microsoft Download Center) at:
  http://www.microsoft.com/en-us/download/details.aspx?id=30160

- Windows Server 2012 NIC Teaming (LBFO) Deployment and Management (Microsoft Download Center) at:
  http://www.microsoft.com/en-us/download/details.aspx?id=30160

Client Hyper-V

We'll end this book with a real-world story of how Jean-Pierre R M de Tiege, a Build Manager with the Government Gateway team at Microsoft, resolved an interesting problem involving Windows 8 Client Hyper-V, wireless networking, and network bridge functionality all running on his laptop.

Wireless networking and network bridge

Having received a new laptop, I decided to install Windows 8 in order to experiment with the OS. After installation, I joined it to the domain from a remote location and created two virtual machines to make use of Hyper-V under Windows 8 and use alternative OS environments, such as Windows 7 and Ubuntu.

After initial success in hooking up these virtual machines through a network adapter to an Ethernet connection, I added a secondary connection to hook up to the wireless network using a network bridge. See the following articles for details:

- Hyper-V: How to Run Hyper-V on a Laptop:
  http://social.technet.microsoft.com/wiki/contents/articles/185.hyper-v-how-to-run-hyper-v-on-a-laptop.aspx
- Making a Wireless Connection Accessible to a Hyper-V Virtual Machine (VM):
  http://blogs.msdn.com/b/donovanf/archive/2011/04/22/making-a-wireless-connection-accessible-to-a-hyper-v-virtual-machine-vm.aspx

The problem

A day after verifying that this worked successfully, I brought the laptop into work and plugged it into the corporate intranet. Once plugged in, the laptop received the full domain policy settings, which, among others restricted the use of network bridges, causing the wireless adapters to no longer function.

The solution

A lot of suggestions on the Internet advocate creating an internal network in Hyper-V and then using Internet connection sharing with the internal network in order to connect to the wireless network adapter. When network bridges are disabled in a domain policy, however, it is usually safe to assume that Internet connection sharing will be disabled as well.

It turns out, however, that deleting the existing virtual switch in Hyper-V and re-creating it by specifically targeting the wireless network adapter of the host environment caused the Windows 8 operating system to automatically create a network bridge that isn't affected by domain policy. Windows 8 utilizes the network bridge internally to allow the wireless network adapter to link up to the Hyper-V adapter and thus bypasses domain policy.

—*Jean-Pierre R M de Tiege, Build Manager, Government Gateway team*

Additional resources

Here is an additional resource concerning this topic:

- Client Hyper-V (TechNet Library) at:
  http://technet.microsoft.com/en-us/library/hh857623.aspx

Now that you've read the book...

Tell us what you think!

Was it useful?
Did it teach you what you wanted to learn?
Was there room for improvement?

Let us know at http://aka.ms/tellpress

Your feedback goes directly to the staff at Microsoft Press, and we read every one of your responses. Thanks in advance!

Microsoft

Lightning Source UK Ltd.
Milton Keynes UK
UKOW06f1140240713

214308UK00016B/34/P